MYSTERIOUS ✦ DEATHS

Malcolm X

These and other titles are included in the *Mysterious Deaths* series:

MYSTERIOUS ✦ DEATHS

Malcolm X

by Miriam Sagan

Lucent Books
P.O. Box 289011, San Diego, CA 92198-9011

Library of Congress Cataloging-in-Publication Data

Sagan, Miriam, 1954–
   Malcolm X / by Miriam Sagan.
      p. cm. — (Mysterious deaths)
   Includes bibliographical references and index.
   Summary: Examines the unanswered questions surrounding the
murder of Malcolm X.
   ISBN 1-56006-264-9 (alk. paper)
   1. X, Malcolm, 1925–1965—Juvenile literature. 2. Black Muslims—
Biography—Juvenile literature. 3. Afro-Americans—Biography—Juvenile
literature. [1. X, Malcolm, 1925–1965—Assassination.] I. Title. II. Series.
BP223Z8L57719   1997
364.1'524'092—dc20   96–43227
                                               CIP
                                               AC

Printed in the U.S.A.
Copyright © 1997 by Lucent Books, Inc.
P.O. Box 289011, San Diego, CA 92198-9011

Contents

Haunting Human History

The *Mysterious Deaths* series focuses on nine individuals whose deaths have never been fully explained. Some are figures from the distant past; others are far more contemporary. Yet all of them remain fascinating as much for who they were and how they lived as for how they died. Their lives were characterized by fame and fortune, tragedy and triumph, secrets that led to acute vulnerability. Our enduring fascination with these stories, then, is due in part to the lives of the victims and in part to the array of conflicting facts and opinions, as well as the suspense, that surrounds their deaths.

Some of the people profiled in the *Mysterious Deaths* series were controversial political figures who lived and died in the public eye. John F. Kennedy, Abraham Lincoln, and Malcolm X were all killed in front of crowds as guards paid to protect them were unable to stop their murders. Despite all precautions, their assassins found ample opportunity to carry out their crimes. In each case, the assassins were tried and convicted. So what remains mysterious? As the reader will discover, everything.

The two women in the series, Marilyn Monroe and Amelia Earhart, are equally well remembered. Both died at the heights of their careers; both, from all appearances, had everything to live for. Yet their deaths have also been shrouded in mystery. While there are simple explanations—Monroe committed suicide, Earhart's plane crashed—the public has never been able to accept them. The more researchers dig into the deaths, the more mysterious evidence they unearth. Monroe's predilection for affairs with prominent politicians may have led to her death. Earhart, brash and cavalier, may have been involved in a government plot that collapsed around her. And these theories do not exhaust the mysterious possibilities that continue to puzzle researchers.

The circumstances of the deaths of the remaining figures in the *Mysterious Deaths* series—Richard III's nephews Edward and

Richard; the brilliant composer Wolfgang Mozart; and the infamous bank robber Butch Cassidy—are less well known but no less fascinating.

For example, what are almost surely the skeletons of the little princes Edward and Richard were found buried at the foot of a stairway in the Tower of London in 1674. To many, the discovery proved beyond a doubt that their evil uncle, Richard III, murdered them to attain the throne. Yet others find Richard wrongly accused, the obvious scapegoat. The mysterious tale of their deaths—full of dungeons, plots, and treachery—is still intriguing today.

In the history books, Wolfgang Mozart died in poverty from a consumptive-like disease. Yet there are reports and rumors, snatches of information culled from distant records, that Mozart may have died from a slow poisoning. Who could have wanted to murder the famous composer? And why?

Finally, bank robber Butch Cassidy's death couldn't have been less mysterious—shot to death by military police in Bolivia along with his companion, the Sundance Kid. Then why did members of Butch Cassidy's family and numerous others swear to have seen him, in full health, in the United States years after his supposed death?

These true-life whodunits are filled with tantalizing "what ifs?" What if Kennedy had used the bulletproof plastic hood that his Secret Servicemen had ready? What if Lincoln had decided not to attend the theater—which he did only to please his wife? What if Monroe's friend, Peter Lawford, receiving no answer to his persistent calls, had gone to her house, as he wanted to do? These questions frustrate us as well as testify to a haunting aspect of human history—the way that seemingly insignificant decisions can alter its course.

A Traumatic Childhood

Malcolm X was born Malcolm Little in Omaha, Nebraska, on May 19, 1925. He was the fourth child of the Reverend Earl Little, a Baptist minister, and Louise Little, who had been born in the British West Indies. Earl Little had three children from a previous marriage, as well. Malcolm also had a younger sister and brother.

Earl Little's controversial beliefs led to constant trouble for his family. Little was a follower of Marcus Garvey, who believed that the descendants of slaves should return to Africa and forge a new life on their ancestral soil. Garvey's focus on autonomy and self-rule for black people inspired fear and hatred in white racists in Omaha, Nebraska.

Because Earl Little preached Garvey to his congregation, he was singled out for persecution by white racists. When Malcolm's mother was pregnant with him, the Ku Klux Klan rode up to the door. Malcolm X opens *The Autobiography of Malcolm X* with an account of the terror his family faced:

> Surrounding the house, brandishing their shotguns and rifles, they shouted for my father to come out. My mother went to the front door and opened it. Standing where they could see her pregnant condition, she told them she was alone with her three small children, and that my father was away preaching, in Milwaukee. The Klansmen shouted threats and warnings to her that we had better get out of town because "the good Christian white people" were not going to stand for my father's "spreading trouble" among the "good" Negroes of Omaha with the "back to Africa" preachings of Marcus Garvey.

The Ku Klux Klan left that night, but the Little family was still targeted for persecution. When the family moved to Lansing, Michigan, so that Earl Little could start his own business, his reputation as an agitator followed him. In 1929 the Littles' house was burned by a Klanlike society of white supremacists who considered Earl Little to be what they called an "uppity nigger."

Malcolm X's earliest memories included this terrifying scene of confusion as the family home burned:

> I remember being suddenly snatched awake into a frightening confusion of pistol shots and shouting and smoke and flames. My father had shouted and shot at the two white men who had set the fire and were running away. Our home was burning down around us. . . . My mother,

Marcus Garvey sought to achieve dignity and civil rights for black people by preaching economic self-sufficiency. Garvey also believed blacks should work toward establishing their own nation in Africa.

The Ku Klux Klan terrorized members of the black community by selectively burning the homes of prominent blacks, especially those they considered "uppity." Malcolm's family was victimized by a Klanlike society when he was a child.

with the baby in her arms, just made it into the yard before the house crashed in, showering sparks. I remember we were outside in the night in our underwear, crying and yelling our heads off.

Although the family survived the fire, when Malcolm was only six years old, his father was run over by a streetcar and killed. The family believed that white supremacists had placed his body under the streetcar tracks to disguise his murder. This violent death was the culmination of years of harassment Earl Little had suffered for his beliefs.

For the next eight years Malcolm's mother, Louise Little, held the family together in extreme poverty. A sensitive and educated woman, she eventually succumbed to the strain and suffered from a nervous breakdown. The breakdown was severe, and Louise Little never recovered, but spent the rest of her life in a psychiatric hospital. From that time on Malcolm, who was only fourteen years old, was raised in foster homes.

Although Malcolm stayed in school throughout these chaotic circumstances, he had his hopes dashed early. In public grade school in Lansing, Malcolm confided to a teacher that he wanted to be a lawyer. "That's no realistic goal for a nigger," the teacher told him. This comment disillusioned Malcolm from continuing his education. Although he graduated from the eighth grade, between the disintegration of his family life and his alienation from the predominantly white school, he did not continue his formal education.

From Street Hustler to Minister

In 1941 Malcolm moved to Boston to live with his half-sister, Ella. The life of the big city intrigued him, and he soon became involved in crime. He sold drugs and committed burglaries. Five years later Malcolm was arrested for burglary of a house. Prison became his home from 1946 until his release in 1952. Paradoxically, it was

A Father's Death

The traumatic death of Malcolm X's father Earl Little left a family fatherless. The events surrounding his father's death were seared into Malcolm's memory, as recounted in The Autobiography of Malcolm X.

"I remember waking up to the sound of my mother's screaming. . . . When I scrambled out, I saw the police in the living room; they were trying to calm her down. And all of us children who were staring knew without anyone having to say it that something terrible had happened to our father.

My mother was taken by the police to the hospital, and to a room where a sheet was over my father in a bed, and she wouldn't look, she was afraid to look. Probably it was wise she didn't. My father's skull, on one side, was crushed in, I was told later. Negroes in Lansing have always whispered that he was attacked, and then laid across some tracks for a streetcar to run over him. His body was cut almost in half. . . .

It was morning when we children at home got word that he was dead. I was six. I can remember a vague commotion, the house filled up with people crying, saying bitterly that the white Black Legion [a local secret society of white supremacists] had finally gotten him. . . .

When we went by the casket, I remember that I thought that it looked as if my father's strong black face had been dusted with flour, and I wished they hadn't put on such a lot of it."

while he was in prison that Malcolm developed the beliefs that would make him a leader.

In prison Malcolm educated himself by reading prodigiously in a wide variety of fields. He also converted to the religion of the Nation of Islam, also known as the Black Muslims. The Nation of Islam is a religious movement led in the United States by Elijah Muhammad. It combines the world religion of Islam with a belief in the superiority of the Black race and of Africans. The Nation of

A Dim View of the Future

In The Autobiography of Malcolm X *by Alex Haley and Malcolm X, Malcolm recounts an incident in the seventh grade when his teacher dashed his hopes for the future.*

"He told me, 'Malcolm, you ought to be thinking about a career. Have you been giving it any thought?' The truth is, I hadn't. I never figured out why I told him, 'Well, yes, sir, I've been thinking I'd like to be a lawyer.'. . . Mr. Ostrowski looked surprised, I remember, and leaned back in his chair and clasped his hands behind his head. He kind of half-smiled and said, 'Malcolm, one of life's first needs is for us to be realistic. Don't misunderstand me now. We all here like you, you know that. But you've got to be realistic about being a nigger. A lawyer—that's no realistic goal for a nigger. You need to think about something you *can* be. You're good with your hands—making things. Everybody admires your carpentry shop work. Why don't you plan on carpentry? People like you as a person—you'd get all kinds of work.'"

Despite, or maybe because of, the ignorant predictions of his teacher, Malcolm X would become one of the most influential blacks of all time.

Elijah Muhammad, leader of the Black Muslims, preaches at a prayer meeting in 1961. Muhammad's message of empowerment and superiority of the black race appealed to many blacks who were experiencing the effects of racism.

Islam's teachings are extremely negative toward white people. One principle of the faith explains that the original races of the world were black and that white people were created by a mad scientist. Malcolm X recounts this story in his *Autobiography:*

> Elijah Muhammad teaches his followers that, first, the moon separated from the earth. Then, the first humans, Original Man, were a black people. They founded the Holy City Mecca. . . . About sixty-six hundred years ago . . . Mr. Yacub was born to create trouble, to break the peace, and to kill. . . . Among many other things, he had learned to breed races scientifically . . . [and he decided] to create upon the earth a devil race—a bleached-out, white race of people.

Malcolm X later rejected Black Muslim stories like this as nonsense, but when he first joined the faith, it spoke to his life experience. Malcolm had certainly experienced the racism of "blue-eyed

Brainwashed by a Blue-Eyed Jesus

When he was in the Nation of Islam, Malcolm X was a fiery speaker who preached on street corners to draw new converts to the Nation. His charismatic style is reflected in this piece from The Autobiography of Malcolm X *by Alex Haley and Malcolm X.*

"Brothers and sisters, the white man has brainwashed us black people to fasten our gaze upon a blond-haired, blue-eyed Jesus! We're worshipping a Jesus that doesn't even *look* like us! Oh, yes! Now just bear with me, listen to the teachings of the Messenger of Allah, the Honorable Elijah Muhammad. Now just think of this. The blond-haired, blue-eyed white man has taught you and me to worship a *white* Jesus, and to sing and shout and pray to this God that's *his* God, the white man's God. The white man has taught us to shout and sing and pray until we *die*, to wait until *death*, for some dreamy heaven-in-the-hereafter, when we're *dead*, while this white man has his milk and honey in the streets paved with golden dollars right here on *this* earth!

You don't believe what I am telling you, brothers and sisters? Well, I'll tell you what you do. You go out of here, you just take a good look around where you live. Look at not only how *you* live, but look at how anybody that you *know* lives—that way, you'll be sure that you're not just a bad-luck accident. And when you get through looking at where *you* live, then you take a walk down across Central Park and start to look at what this white God has brought to the white man. I mean, take yourself a look down there at how the white man is living!"

devils." Black Muslims also preached the dream of a separate nation for Black people, whether in North America or Africa. This was reminiscent of the philosophy of Marcus Garvey, in whom Malcolm had always believed.

While still in prison, Malcolm wrote to Elijah Muhammad and began to diligently study his teachings. When he was released in 1952, Malcolm went directly to Detroit to live with his brother, Wilfred, who was a devout Black Muslim. Malcolm began attending the religion's Detroit temple and living according to the principles of the Muslims, such as not eating pork, praying at set times throughout the day, abstaining from drugs and alcohol, and emphasizing the importance of marriage and child-rearing. Malcolm threw himself wholeheartedly into this new life. He applied to be officially accepted by the Nation of Islam, which involved dropping his last name, Little, and receiving in its place an X.

> The Muslim's "X" symbolized the true African family name that he never could know. For me, my "X" replaced the white slavemaster name of "Little," which some blue-eyed devil named Little had imposed upon my paternal forebears [ancestors]. The receipt of my "X" meant that forever after in the nation of Islam, I would be known as Malcolm X.

Malcolm X's name would change again, after he became an adherent of more orthodox Islam and had made a pilgrimage to Mecca. At that point he would take Shabazz as his family name, and this was the name by which his wife and daughters would be known.

Malcolm X became a committed organizer for the Nation of Islam. He built up the membership in the Detroit temple, recruiting from the bars, poolrooms, and streetcorners of the Detroit ghetto. Malcolm's former life on the street and his experiences in prison made him sensitive to the problems of poor African Americans. In 1953 he was named assistant minister to Detroit's Temple One. As for Elijah Muhammad, Malcolm X felt he owed him his life, both spiritually and in actuality. He said of Elijah Muhammad, simply, "I worshipped him."

Malcolm X's family life also stabilized within the Nation of Islam when in 1958 he married Betty Sanders, later known as Betty Shabazz. The same year, a daughter, Atallah, was born to them; in 1960 their daughter, Qubilah, was born. The third of Malcolm's daughters, Ityasah, was born in 1962, and the fourth, Gamilah, was born two years later. Much as Malcolm X loved his family, he was increasingly busy traveling, speaking, and fund-raising for the Nation of Islam. Malcolm X began his rise to national prominence as a spokesman for the Nation of Islam. He was a charismatic speaker and organizer who understood the lives of African Americans who were attracted to the religion. Malcolm X established new temples and helped others grow in membership. Throughout this period, he worked intimately with his mentor, Elijah Muhammad. But

Betty Shabazz married Malcolm X in 1958 and also embraced the Black Muslims. Both she and Malcolm would raise their children in the tenets of the Black Muslims.

Malcolm X's prominence in the Nation of Islam was not without its problems. Elijah Muhammad once told him, "Brother Malcolm, I want you to become well known, because if you are well known, it will make *me* better known." But then he continued, "Brother Malcolm, there is something you need to know. You will grow to be hated when you become well known. Because usually people get jealous of public figures." And in retrospect Malcolm X himself was to observe, "Nothing that Mr. Muhammad ever said to me was more prophetic."

A Break with the Nation

By 1963, Malcolm X began to doubt Elijah Muhammad's legitimacy as a religious leader. This stemmed from the fact that Elijah Muhammad did not practice what he preached. The Nation of Islam preaches a strict morality, including dedication to family and marital fidelity. Elijah Muhammad had violated his own code. Several women accused him of fathering children out of wedlock with them. Malcolm X was close enough to the daily workings of Elijah Muhammad's office and household to know that the accusations were true. Others in the religious hierarchy hushed up the affairs, not wanting a scandal to rock or destroy the Nation. For Malcolm X, Elijah Muhammad's actions were deeply disillusioning. Malcolm also disagreed with Elijah Muhammad on the role Black Muslims should play in the Civil Rights Movement. Malcolm thought Black Muslims should take a leading role, while Elijah Muhammad believed they should stay out of politics. The breach between the two increased until 1964, when Elijah Muhammad censured Malcolm X by publicly suspending him as a minister and

Malcolm X with Elijah Muhammad in 1961. Although Malcolm rose to a leadership role in the Black Muslims, he became disillusioned with Elijah Muhammad—especially when he found that Muhammad did not practice the tenets he preached.

silencing him—that is, forbidding him to speak in public. Malcolm and his family were living at that time in a house owned by the Nation of Islam. As part of the falling-out between Malcolm X and Elijah Muhammad, the Nation attempted to evict Malcolm's family. At this point, Malcolm X began to see that he might need to irrevocably leave Elijah Muhammad. He began to think about building an organization of his own, one

> which would help to challenge the American black man to gain his human rights, and to cure his mental, spiritual, economic, and political sicknesses. . . . Substantially, as I saw it, the organization I hoped to build would differ from the Nation of Islam in that it would embrace all faiths of black men, and it would carry into practice what the Nation of Islam had only preached.

Many of Malcolm's followers in the Nation indicated that if he left, they would leave. This presented a direct threat to the Nation of Islam. Malcolm remembers:

> Each day, more militant . . . brothers who had been with me in Mosque Seven announced their break from the Nation of Islam to come with me. And each day, I learned in one way or another, of more support from non-Muslim Negroes. . . . There was a growing clamor: "When are you going to call a meeting, to get organized?"

But before Malcolm X was ready to build his own organization in direct opposition to the Nation, he felt the need to learn more about the traditional world religion of Islam. He continued to strengthen his faith by making a pilgrimage to Mecca in 1964. Mecca is the holy city that is the spiritual heart of the Muslim world. On this pilgrimage Malcolm learned more about the traditional Muslim religion, which was far more tolerant than the Nation of Islam. Traditional Muslims welcomed worshippers of all races and backgrounds and emphasized the spirit of brotherhood and love as well as the existence of one God, Allah, who is also identified as the god of the Christians and the Jews. Malcolm was impressed by what he saw at Mecca: "The *brotherhood*! The people of all races, colors, from all over the world coming together as *one*! It has proved to me the power of the One God." The experience was to lead to a new tolerance in Malcolm toward people of all colors.

Malcolm X returns to the United States after visiting the Middle East in 1964. Malcolm X experienced an epiphany after visiting the Holy Land, breaking away from the Nation of Islam and its message of hate and separation of the races.

After Mecca Malcolm went on to visit many of the new and emerging nations of Africa. He did this in the same spirit as his pilgrimage—to discover a larger political and spiritual context for the organization he hoped to build back home. The new countries of Africa had thrown off colonial governments and were now practicing self-rule. They were an inspiration to Malcolm because they no longer depended on European governments but were pursuing the same ideal of self-sufficiency that Marcus Garvey had preached. Many of these countries had socialist economies and shared an ideal of pan-African unity. For Malcolm it was an inspiration to see countries run by Black men and women.

His visits included Egypt, Nigeria, the Sudan, Ghana, Liberia, Senegal, and Morocco. He talked with ambassadors at their embassies, often discussing the problems of African Americans in the United States. He was greeted with interest and admiration. When he returned from his trips to Mecca and Africa, Malcolm X was ready to start building his own organization, one that embraces the ideal of brotherhood rather than the strict segregation of the Nation of Islam.

So in 1964, the year of his international travels, Malcolm X broke off firmly and publicly with Elijah Muhammad and the Nation of Islam to organize his own Organization of Afro-American Unity.

The Nation of Islam did not take kindly to Malcolm's defection, because it justifiably feared that Malcolm would take a large part of the membership with him. In *Muhammad Speaks*, the newspaper of the Nation of Islam, Malcolm was called "an international hobo" and threatened, "You are now the target of both your own

Malcolm X cautiously emerges from his car after a firebomb was tossed into his house in 1965. Malcolm believed that the Nation of Islam was behind the act.

followers (which are very few) and the followers of Muhammad." Elijah Muhammad himself attacked him in the same paper: "I will never forget this hypocrite's disgraceful acts against me. . . . I shall remind him of his evil and wicked acts done to me in return for the good I did him."

After Malcolm left the Nation of Islam, he began to receive death threats. A Black Muslim told a close follower of Malcolm's, "You fell in love with that . . . nigger, but we're going to kill him." Another friend of Malcolm's, still in the Nation, was approached by four Muslims looking for a pistol silencer so they could kill Malcolm. At the end of January in 1965, Malcolm left his house and found three Muslims waiting for him. There was a scuffle, and they fled. Malcolm was well aware of the threats against him and went so far as to tell a police detective that he was convinced the Black Muslims would assassinate him in a public place and that "it's only going to be a matter of time."

On February 14, 1965, Malcolm's house was firebombed and burned as his family slept. No one was killed, but four days later the family was formally evicted by the Nation of Islam. By this time Malcolm seemed convinced that the Black Muslims would soon kill him. Talking to the *New York Times*, Malcolm X said simply, "I live like a man who's already dead. I'm a marked man. . . . This thing with me will be resolved by death and violence." He told a friend, Edward Bradley, "I am a marked man. I'm ready to die. I just don't want them to hurt my family."

1 The Murder of Malcolm X

The six-hundred-seat Audubon Ballroom in the Harlem section of New York City was crowded the winter afternoon of February 21, 1965. A large crowd of men and women, predominantly African-American, had come to hear Malcolm X about his new group, the Organization of Afro-American Unity.

The crowd was composed mostly of Malcolm's supporters. But it also contained some curious visitors, including former and current members of the Nation of Islam. Unknown to Malcolm, an undercover police officer was also in the audience, but he was not there to protect Malcolm; rather, Gene Roberts had been infiltrating Malcolm's new organization for the FBI. And in the friendly and expectant crowd a handful of men sat silently, weapons concealed, waiting for their moment to arrive.

When Malcolm arrived at the Audubon Hotel on upper Broadway in Harlem, a lone police officer stood at the front entrance. Usually at the start of one of Malcolm's speeches, the sidewalk and entrance of a building would have had somewhere between five and several dozen officers standing in attendance. But today one of Malcolm's own security men had asked the captain on duty to take his officers off the door and put them somewhere else. The captain complied. Two policemen in uniform were then stationed out of sight in the Rose Ballroom, next to the room in which Malcolm was speaking. An additional twenty men were placed across the street at the Columbia Presbyterian Medical Center, where they were completely hidden from view.

Malcolm X, as well as his own security force, did not want the police within the hall. Several weeks before his death, Malcolm had called off the routine security checks in which people were searched for weapons at his meetings. These checks had irritated his followers, who felt their loyalty was being called into question.

Besides, the security checks were a remnant of the style of the Nation, which Malcolm had left behind. Malcolm had said, "If I can't be safe among my own kind, where can I be?" For the same reason, Malcolm and his security people felt that the white police force was an unwelcome presence at a peaceful meeting of Malcolm's new organization. Malcolm's security force must also have felt that they could easily take care of any problems themselves.

The New York City police were glad to move from the Audubon Ballroom. As a rule they did not like the radical Malcolm X and feared the effect he might have if he chose to instigate a crowd of his followers. A senior police officer told a reporter, off the record, that Malcolm was "vicious" and continued, "I'm not a Negro. I'm not going to follow him, I'm going to fight him."

Malcolm's security team, however, was unusually lax that day at the Audubon. Usually his security team was a notable and lethal

Crowds jam the sidewalks outside the Audubon Ballroom to hear Malcolm X speak of his new religious philosophy. Many security precautions usually taken by Malcolm were ignored on this day.

presence with many members trained in the martial arts. However, on that February day Malcolm's own guards were not as rigorous as usual. Dozens of people were seated in the ballroom before the guards arrived. And as the security checks were no longer enforced, several men in the audience had brought in guns. Even a Black Muslim wearing an identifying pin in his lapel, who would normally be turned away as a man hostile to Malcolm, was seated.

Premonitions of Death

Shortly before two o'clock in the afternoon, Malcolm X was backstage, preparing for his speech. Although Malcolm was usually a calm and jovial man, often joking with those around him, today he seemed tense and preoccupied. Benjamin Goodman, his chief aide, said later, "He was more tense than I'd ever seen him, and I'd seen him for seven years. He just lost control of himself completely. I never saw him do that before." It was as if Malcolm had a premonition that he was in danger. He had recently told his lawyer, "You can run and run and run, but when the time comes, you are going to die."

In *The Autobiography of Malcolm X*, he told coauthor Alex Haley: "To come right down to it, if I take the kind of things in which I believe then add to that the kind of temperament that I have, plus the one hundred percent dedication I have to whatever I believe in—these are ingredients which make it just about impossible for me to die of old age."

Although Malcolm had premonitions of a violent death, he was unclear about who might kill him. By 1965 his enemies included the Nation of Islam, and he was also unpopular among the power structure of New York City and the federal government, which considered him a dangerous rabble-rouser.

Just before he went on stage at the Audubon, Malcolm said, "The way I feel, I ought not to go out there today." A few minutes after 2 P.M., Benjamin Goodman stepped on stage to introduce Malcolm X to the crowd. He could not have known how unfortunately prophetic his words were: "I present . . . one who is willing to put himself on the line for you, . . . a man who would give his life for you."

The audience applauded as Malcolm stepped out smiling. "*Assalaam alaikum*," he said, using the Muslim greeting, "Peace be with you." The crowd responded, "*Wa-alaikum salaam*" (and with you).

Malcolm X had premonitions that he would not lead a long life. He told Claude Lewis, an African-American reporter quoted in Peter Goldman's book, The Death and Life of Malcolm X:

"I'll never get old. . . . If you read, you'll find that very few people who think like I think live long enough to get old. When I say by any means necessary, I mean it with all my heart, my mind and my soul. A black man should give his life to be free, and he should also be willing to take the life of those who want to take his. When you really think like that, you don't live long. So I never think about being an old man. That never has come across my mind. I can't even see myself old . . . [but I would like to be remembered as] *Sincere.* In whatever I did or do. Even if I made mistakes, they were made in sincerity. If I'm wrong, I'm wrong in sincerity. I think the best thing that a person can be is sincere."

Almost immediately the greetings of peace were interrupted by a commotion in the crowd. According to Peter Goldman, who interviewed witnesses, two men in the audience began to quarrel loudly with one another. "What are you doing in my pockets, man? Get your hands out of my pocket," one said to the other as the two began to scuffle with each other. Gene Roberts, the undercover police officer, moved toward them. Malcolm, from the stage, was telling the men to "Hold it, hold it, brothers, let's be cool." Malcolm's security guards moved toward the men to try to quiet the scuffle.

The roar of a shotgun deafened the ears of those in the ballroom. A dozen double-O buckshot pellets ripped through the plywood lectern that ineffectually shielded Malcolm's body. The shotgun blasted a seven-inch circle of holes in the exact center of Malcolm's chest.

Malcolm tried to bring his hands up to his face. Blood coursed down his shirt. Malcolm's eyes rolled back in his head. He fell backward, at first breaking his fall on two empty chairs behind him. Then he crashed to the floor.

Malcolm X is given first aid after being shot in the Audubon Ballroom. All attempts to save his life would fail.

The assassin with the shotgun fired again. Two more black men appeared out of the crowd, one shooting a Luger pistol and one holding a .45 automatic pistol. These two gunmen shot again and again into Malcolm X's dying body.

A Scene of Chaos

The scene in the audience was one of terror and confusion as people tried to scatter. Some yelled, "It's a bomb! It's a bomb!" Others, realizing what had happened, shouted "They shot Malcolm! They shot Malcolm!" Men and women dove for cover, husbands tried to shield their wives, parents their children. Betty Shabazz, Malcolm's wife, was pregnant with twins at the time. She had just arrived with three of their four little girls and was trying to get them out of their snowsuits. When the shots rang out, Betty threw the girls under a coat and covered them with her body, trying to protect them from whatever was happening.

Malcolm's bodyguards began to fire back at the two men shooting in front of Malcolm and what appeared to be one or two additional gunmen firing from the side of the room. The gunmen turned to make their escape. So did the two men who had started the fake altercation in the crowd as a planned distraction.

The man with the Luger was thrown down the stairs by a supporter of Malcolm's, but he managed to escape from the ballroom. The man with the shotgun also vanished. Of the four or five possible assassins, only one was actually captured at the scene of the crime. Reuben X, also known as Reuben Francis, one of Malcolm's bodyguards, shot the man holding the .45 and managed to wound him in the leg. This man was twenty-two-year-old Talmadge Hayer. Even with a bullet in his leg, he hopped out of the building. But as soon as he appeared on the street, the crowd realized he was one of the gunmen who had shot Malcolm; they attacked him, breaking one of his legs.

"Shots fired, Audubon Ballroom!" yelled New York City patrolman Henry into his walkie-talkie. He and patrolman Carroll were stationed next door in the Rose Ballroom and not at the scene. The policemen ran into the Audubon Ballroom with their .38s drawn but were too late to prevent the shooting of Malcolm X.

Meanwhile, out on the pavement, patrolman Thomas Hoy pulled Talmadge Hayer from the mob that was beating him. Two other New York City policemen wrestled him into a squad car.

While Hayer was being reckoned with, Malcolm himself lay on the stage, his life ebbing away. A nurse rushed toward him and tried to give him mouth-to-mouth resuscitation. So did Gene Roberts. When she realized what was going on, Betty Shabazz began to scream, "They're killing my husband!" On her knees next to Malcolm she could see his face go ashen.

Immediately a group of Malcolm's supporters rushed across the street to the Columbia Presbyterian Medical Center. They grabbed a stretcher and an intern and rushed back for Malcolm. Despite their haste, Malcolm X was dead by the time he arrived at the emergency room. The shotgun blast had destroyed his heart and lungs.

By now the street outside the hospital was crowded with reporters and people anxious to hear a word about Malcolm's condition. Their hopes were shattered by the blunt words of a hospital spokesman who announced, "The gentleman you know as Malcolm X is dead."

Police wheel Malcolm X from the Audubon Ballroom on a stretcher after he is shot. Malcolm would be mourned worldwide.

Burial of a Black Prince

Malcolm's friends and followers, and of course his wife and daughters, began the sad process of burying and mourning the man they had loved. News of the assassination reverberated nationally, as African-American leaders across the country praised him. Malcolm was mourned even internationally, particularly in the emerging nations he had admired. The *Daily Times* of Lagos, Nigeria, wrote: "He was a dedicated and consistent disciple of the movement for the emancipation of his brethren.... Malcolm X has fought and died for what he believed to be right." And a newspaper in Ghana, the *Daily Graphic*, eulogized, "The assassination of Malcolm X will go down in history as the greatest blow the American integrationist movement has suffered since the shocking assassination of Medgar Evers and John F. Kennedy."

But it was the neighborhoods of Harlem in New York City that mourned the most. Harlem was Malcolm X's adopted home and one of the largest African-American communities in the United States. Stores were closed and handwritten notes of grief adorned storefront windows. At the Unity Funeral Home in Harlem, Malcolm's body was displayed to a grieving crowd. So many people wanted to pay their last respects that the line wound for several hours outside the funeral home despite the freezing cold. Malcolm's body lay on display until the end of the week; thirty thousand people came to say farewell to the man they had admired and respected as a leader of their community.

Civic and civil rights leaders were concerned that the assassination of Malcolm X would cause a full-scale war to erupt between

A bar in Harlem announces that it is closed to honor Malcolm X on the day of his burial, February 27, 1965. Malcolm's death was felt most severely in Harlem, one of the largest black communities in the United States.

his followers and the Black Muslims. James Farmer, national director of the civil rights organization Congress of Racial Equality (CORE), went so far as to suggest that Malcolm had been killed by a third party who wanted such violence to occur: "Malcolm's murder was calculated to produce more violence and murder and vengeance killings." At the funeral home security was tight. But despite several bomb threats from unknown sources that led to two

"I Know that I Could Suddenly Die"

In the last months of his life, Malcolm X felt he was a marked man. He was sure that the Nation of Islam wanted him dead. He bluntly told this to Alex Haley in The Autobiography of Malcolm X:

"Every morning when I wake up, now, I regard it as having another borrowed day. In any city, wherever I go, making speeches, holding meetings of my organization, or attending to other business, black men are watching every move I make, awaiting their chance to kill me. I have said publicly many times that I know they have their orders. Anyone who chooses not to believe what I am saying doesn't know the Muslims in the Nation of Islam. . . .

I know, too, that I could suddenly die at the hands of some white racists. Or I could die at the hands of some Negro hired by the white man. Or it could be some brainwashed Negro acting on his own idea that by eliminating me he would be helping out the white man, because I talk about the white man the way I do.

Anyway, now, each day I live as if I am already dead, and I tell you what I would like for you to do. When I *am* dead—I say it that way because from the things I *know*, I do not expect to live long enough to read this [autobiography] in its finished form—I want you to just watch and see if I'm not right in what I say: That the white man, in his press, is going to identify me with "hate."

. . . (But) if I can die having brought any light, having exposed any meaningful truth that will help to destroy the racist cancer that is malignant in the body of America—then, all of the credit is due to Allah. Only the mistakes have been mine."

Graveside prayers are offered at Malcolm's funeral. Betty Shabazz, Malcolm's wife, stands at right. Even after his death, Malcolm X's family and followers were further harassed when his church was firebombed shortly after his assassination.

complete police searches of the premises, no violence erupted at the Unity Funeral Home. Several men were arrested for carrying concealed weapons on their way to Malcolm's viewing, potentially averting a violent scene.

However, Malcolm's death was not without repercussions. Eleven hours after Malcolm X was murdered, the Nation of Islam's Mosque Seven at 116th Street and Lenox Avenue was burned by arson. This was the mosque that Malcolm X had run for ten years as a minister with the Nation of Islam. An explosion ripped through the building and fire leapt thirty feet into the air. It took seven hours for firemen to quench the flames, and six firefighters were injured beneath a wall of fire. Although it was never officially proven, New York City police and Harlemites alike knew that the five-alarm fire had been set by Malcolm's followers in retaliation for his murder. There was also an attempt at arson made at a Nation of Islam mosque in San Francisco. Burning a mosque was obviously not on the same scale as killing a human being, but Malcolm's followers wanted to show the Nation of Islam that their

A Eulogy for the Prince

The well-known African-American actor, Ossie Davis, gave the moving eulogy for Malcolm X. The speech is quoted in The Autobiography of Malcolm X.

"Here—at this final hour, in this quiet place, Harlem has come to bid farewell to one of its brightest hopes—extinguished now, and gone from us forever. . . .

Many will ask what Harlem finds to honor in this stormy, controversial and bold young captain—and we will smile. . . . They will say he is of hate—a fanatic, a racist—who can only bring evil to the cause for which you struggle!

And we will answer and say unto them: Did you ever talk to brother Malcolm? Did you ever touch him, or have him smile at you? Did you ever really listen to him? Did he ever do a mean thing? Was he ever himself associated with violence or public disturbance? For if you did you would know him. And if you knew him you would know why we must honor him: Malcolm was our manhood, our living, black manhood! This was his meaning to his people. And, in honoring him, we honor the best in ourselves. . . . And we will know him then for what he was and is—a Prince—our own black shining Prince!— who didn't hesitate to die, because he loved us so."

Actor Ossie Davis delivers a eulogy for Malcolm X. Davis called Malcolm "our own black shining Prince."

religious sanctuaries were no longer safe. But a full-scale war did not erupt between Malcolm's followers and the Nation.

Malcolm X was buried on Saturday, February 27. He was wrapped in a traditional white Islamic shroud, his face peaceful above the flowing cloth. A thousand people attended the funeral at the Faith Temple Church of God while three thousand waited outside. The eulogy was given by African-American actor and director Ossie Davis, who called Malcolm X "our own black shining Prince! . . . who didn't hesitate to die, because he loved us so."

Malcolm X was buried with Islamic rites at the Ferncliff Cemetery outside of New York City in Westchester County under his full Islamic name: el-Hajj Malik el-Shabazz. The grave diggers stood aside as Malcolm's followers began to cover his coffin with dirt, a last show of support and love for the fallen man.

Malcolm X was dead and buried. The world had seen his dying face twisted in a grimace of pain in black-and-white photos in the newspaper. After death, the name of Malcolm X would ring with the controversy and confusion surrounding his murder. In the days after his death, ensuing events would create even more unanswered questions in the minds of police investigators, Malcolm's followers, and family.

2 The Investigation Leads to Unanswered Questions

The New York City police looked for suspects in the assassination of Malcolm X. Of course one man was already in custody, Talmadge Hayer, who had been caught at the scene of the crime. But the police were convinced that at least two, and possibly more, assassins were involved in the murder. The crime had occurred in front of hundreds of witnesses, and the New York City police tried to interview as many of the eyewitnesses as possible. The police asked about the number of shots they heard, the number of assassins, and what the gunmen looked like. However, the detective work was difficult because many of the witnesses were either former Black Muslims or simply African Americans who did not believe in cooperating with the white police force. Indeed, many of the witnesses were so suspicious of the police that they doubted that the police had had any interest in preventing or investigating the shooting of Malcolm X.

The witnesses were not only hostile to the police, but the chaos in the Audubon Ballroom produced differing eyewitness accounts. One of the police investigators described the problems with the detective work to Peter Goldman:

> The problem was to try to piece together from this confusing mass of detail what had actually occurred. The murder took place in front of perhaps two hundred witnesses and, as you know, no two people ever see the same thing the same way. The second problem was that the prospective witnesses were people who were not partial to the authorities.

Still, the detective continued, the eyewitnesses were the important starting point for the police investigation. "The one saving grace was that, by and large, the people in the ballroom were absolutely devoted to Malcolm X. We received quite a lot of cooperation from his followers, who were sincerely interested in finding out who had killed him and bringing those responsible to justice."

The New York City police assumed that Malcolm X had been killed by Black Muslims. After all, members of the Nation of Islam had made documented threats against him for a year and were the main suspects in the firebombing of his house. Elijah Muhammad himself was not investigated by the police, and he tried to distance himself and his followers from being implicated in Malcolm's death. Elijah Muhammad told Peter Goldman: "I don't have any knowledge of anyone trying to kill Malcolm. We have never resorted to such a thing as violence." And he continued, "Malcolm

No Excuse to Riot

Various leaders in the African-American community tried to prevent a violent confrontation between Malcolm's followers and the Black Muslims. Quoted by Michael Friedly in Malcolm X: The Assassination, *James Shabazz, one of Malcolm's followers, counseled:*

"If this becomes a war of black man against black man, Muslim against Muslim, who benefits? The followers of Mr. Muhammad do not, nor do the loyal supporters of Malcolm. The only ones who benefit are those elements who have enslaved us, kept us in slavery and who seek to perpetuate us in slavery. I, respecting the thinking, accomplishments and determinations of Malcolm X, am concerned with the unification of all people of African origin in America and the rest of the world."

And an editorial in Harlem's New York Amsterdam News, *quoted in the same book, warned that:*

"None of these . . . emotions [from Malcolm X's death] can be, or should be used as an excuse to set off disorder and rioting such as took place in our community a few months ago. Despite what has been said about him, Malcolm X had a great respect for law and order and no one can truthfully say that he ever precipitated a riot, or was ever known to lead one. . . . Let's give Malcolm the warmth and respect that is due him. But let's be cool about it!"

died of his own preaching. He preached violence, and violence took him away." Yet despite Elijah Muhammad's disavowals, his newspaper, *Muhammad Speaks*, had called Malcolm X a "chief hypocrite" who was "worthy of death."

Because the New York City police believed Malcolm had been assassinated by Black Muslims, they looked for suspects who were known to be Muslim enforcers, that is, men who would issue a threat of violence or carry out violence on orders from someone high in the Muslim hierarchy. The New York City police got their

Norman Butler was arrested in connection with Malcolm X's assassination. Butler was the second man to be arrested for the slaying.

first break in the case when they began to investigate a similar assassination attempt. A Black Muslim named Benjamin Brown had also left the Nation of Islam to found a rival organization. After some threats from the Muslims, Brown was shot in the back but recovered in the hospital and was able to identify his would-be assassins.

Detective John Kilroy noticed that descriptions of Malcolm X's assassins matched two of the three men who had shot Benjamin Brown. The method of the crime had also been similar. The police made their first move against Norman Butler of the Bronx. Butler was a member of the Fruit of Islam, the paramilitary guards of the Nation of Islam. Butler had been out on bail from the Brown case when Malcolm X was killed. He was soon a prime suspect in the case.

The police questioned Norman Butler for four hours about the shooting of Malcolm X. "I didn't kill him," Butler insisted to Peter Goldman. But at least two eyewitnesses from the Audubon Ballroom were able to identify Butler. He was taken to the Tombs, New York City's notorious jail, where he was held without bail.

Police next arrested Thomas Johnson. Johnson was a member of the Fruit of Islam and a suspect in the shooting of Benjamin Brown. The police were greatly aided by one of Malcolm's bodyguards, Cary Thomas, who came forward as a star witness. It was only with Thomas's testimony that the police were truly able to build a case against the Black Muslim suspects. Thomas was able to identify all three suspects—Talmadge Hayer, Norman Butler, and Thomas Johnson—as the men who had assassinated Malcolm X.

Cary Thomas was the major witness for the police. The police could verify that he had been on the scene, thanks to some photographs taken after the shooting. His testimony fit the police hypothesis that paid assassins had been ordered to kill Malcolm X. Also, no other major witnesses had volunteered to work with the police. However, the police did have questions about Thomas's reliability. Cary Thomas was a former junkie and dope dealer whose testimony was not always consistent. Although Cary Thomas was innocent of any crime, the police decided to jail him as a material witness to ensure that Thomas would not leave town before the trial and to protect him from a possible murder attempt by the Black Muslims.

Enthusiastic Recruits

Two of the suspects held by the police in the slaying of Malcolm X readily admitted to being Black Muslims but claimed to have no animosity toward Malcolm X. Both Norman Butler and Thomas Johnson contended that they were innocent of the assassination of Malcolm X. Butler became interested in the Nation of Islam in 1959, when he was serving in the U.S. Navy. When he first read a Black Muslim newspaper, he was immediately attracted to the Nation of Islam. Butler recollected, "So I read the paper and I said, 'Wow! This is great.' And I wrote them. So the letter came back from (Nation of Islam) headquarters, 'If you still feel the same way when you get out of the military service, come to the mosque.'" In this quote from Friedly's Malcolm X: The Assassination, *Butler, who eventually became a member of the Fruit of Islam, expresses his enthusiasm for the Black Muslim teachings.*

"After I read . . . how the women were treated [with respect] and how women acted, all that stuff was good to me, because that's what I was about, y' know? I was about discipline in the first place, been in the service for five years, and I was about certain things. My attitude was in a certain way. Not necessarily against whites but for black. Or for the elevation and the advancement of black. So that's how come I became a Muslim. Not because of Elijah Muhammad, and I had never *heard* of Malcolm X."

Thomas Johnson, also quoted by Friedly and also a member of the Fruit of Islam, was drawn to the Black Muslims because of Malcolm X, the man he was later accused of killing:

"I used to listen to him on the radio—used to have him on . . . talk shows . . . and I used to get a lot of delight out of the way he used to handle himself. . . .

I couldn't figure out why he would do something like [leave the Black Muslims], y' know, against the teaching [of Elijah Muhammad]. It upset me. But I'm the type of person, man, that I don't get emotional. I think things out. . . . I don't become inflamed."

Thomas Johnson is booked by police in connection with the assassination of Malcolm X. He was the third suspect arrested.

On March 10, 1965, with the help of Thomas's testimony, the grand jury indicted Hayer, Butler, and Johnson on the charge that they had "Willfully, feloniously and of malice aforethought shot and killed Malcolm Little, aka Malcolm X, with shotgun and pistols." This meant that the three men would now stand trial for the murder of Malcolm X.

The Suspects and Accomplices

The New York City police now had three suspects in the shooting. The ballistics department examined the evidence from the crime and deduced that three guns had been used. However, witnesses at the scene in the Audubon Ballroom reported seeing up to five assassins. Were two men missing from the police roundup and indictment?

The New York City police wanted to settle the case quickly. One detective described to Peter Goldman, "Okay, now you got three guys locked up, and all you have to do then is prove the case on each of them, plus prove the case of association between them."

Six detectives worked on the case for ten months from the arrests to trial and then through the trial itself. The detectives continued to question witness after witness, even paying cash for information. One detective said, "I put out maybe a thousand dollars for stoolies. A case like that can put you in the poorhouse."

The police work, however, turned up no further suspects. So the detectives settled on creating a case around the three suspects that they already had safely behind bars. The official police case would be that Hayer, Butler, and Johnson had been the only men involved in killing Malcolm X. Some investigators estimated the number of men involved in the shooting to be from four to seven but could dig up no hard proof to substantiate this. The investigators assumed that there had been three gunmen, probably two people who created the staged diversion, and at least one driver for a getaway car. Obviously Hayer, Butler, and Johnson were only three men, leaving up to four suspects at large. These suspects were never identified, questioned, or brought to trial. They remain, to this day, mystery men. As one investigating detective

The Audubon Ballroom, the scene of Malcolm X's assassination. Police investigators built their prosecution around the three suspects that they were able to arrest, although they did not think they had gotten all the participants in the assassination.

summed up years later when he spoke to Peter Goldman, author of *The Death and Life of Malcolm X*, "I'm satisfied we had the three gunmen. I'm not satisfied that we had everybody involved."

Another problem for the police, even with their working hypothesis about the assassination and three suspects in custody, was the underlying question: Who was the mastermind behind the shooting of Malcolm X? Surely Hayer, Butler, and Johnson had not been working in some random way, and none of the three had any personal grudge against Malcolm X. Butler and Johnson were both quite active as Black Muslims. The police felt sure that the order to shoot Malcolm had come from higher up in the Nation of Islam than the enforcers themselves.

One of the detectives stated the Black Muslim motive as simply the fact that "Malcolm was drawing off Black Muslims [into his own organization]. . . . He was cutting both sides of the cake. He would have busted the Black Muslim empire completely apart." But who had given the order to pull the trigger? The police believed that Hayer, Butler, and Johnson were paid assassins who had shot Malcolm X for a fee. One said, "We were dealing with paid assassins and they weren't giving anybody above them up. You can believe, feel, *know*, but that isn't legal proof." However, this investigator's hunch was never proven in a court of law, leaving the question open. It was a question that would still haunt Malcolm's family and the African-American community thirty years after Malcolm X's death.

Bodyguards Under Suspicion

The New York City police also believed that it was possible that some of Malcolm's own men had set up the assassination. The police pointed to the lax security surrounding the Audubon Ballroom on that fateful day. It had been suspiciously easy for the killers to enter the scene. An investigator aired his suspicion to reporter Peter Goldman: "To us, it was all so—*perfect.*" To the police, the shooting of Malcolm X had just been too easy to accomplish. The detective continued that the assassins would not have simply walked in and shot Malcolm unless they knew that they could get away with it and had at least one of Malcolm's own security men working for them: "Nobody would have walked in there to shoot him unless you know nobody has a gun [unless he was sure no one else had a gun] and unless you know you've got one key man in your pocket."

The Audubon Ballroom after being roped off by police. The police investigators found that many of the security precautions normally taken by Malcolm's followers were either ignored or forgotten on the day of his assassination.

In his book, Peter Goldman quotes a police investigator who found the fact that Malcolm's security guards were not carrying guns and did not search the members of the audience suspicious, too:

> Generally, Malcolm's bodyguards carried guns, but this particular day he supposedly said no. Nobody was searched— that supposedly was from Malcolm, too. Somebody tells the duty captain that they don't want the policemen visible; he said *that* came from Malcolm X. Of course, Malcolm X was dead, and we can't question him. Normally there were at least four people on the stage with him, but this time, nobody. I think the word was given to stay away. And how do those three guys [the assassins] get in? These were men who were known to Malcolm's followers; they shouldn't have been in there, or if they were, they should have been searched. I mean, it all worked *too* smoothly. It was incredible that these things could have all happened in one day.

Two Leaders, Two Martyrs

During their lives, Malcolm X and Dr. Martin Luther King Jr. met only once. Although they were both completely dedicated to improving the lives of African Americans, their methods were completely different. Dr. Martin Luther King abhorred the use of violence and followed the pacifist teachings of Mohandas Gandhi. Malcolm X preached that improvement was necessary "by whatever means possible" and felt that Black people should defend themselves.

However, after their deaths, both King and Malcolm X were seen as martyrs to the cause who had been murdered by a society full of racism and violence. This excerpt from Malcolm X: The Assassination *is taken from a press conference given by Martin Luther King Jr. on Malcolm X's assassination on February 24, 1965.*

"The assassination of Malcolm X was an unfortunate tragedy and it reveals that there are still numerous people in our nation who have degenerated to the point of expressing murder, and we haven't learned to disagree without being violently disagreeable. . . . I think one must understand that in condemning the philosophy of Malcolm X, which I did constantly, that he was a victim of the despair that came into being as a result of a society that gives so many negroes the nagging sense of 'nobodyness.' And just as one condemns the philosophy, he must be as vigorous in condemning the continued existence in our society of the conditions of racial injustice, depression and man's inhumanity to man."

Malcolm X shakes hands with Martin Luther King Jr. Both would sacrifice their lives in the struggle for civil rights.

Other police officers, however, doubted that Malcolm had been betrayed by his own security men. They felt that it just was not that difficult for the assassins to enter the Audubon Ballroom and complete their murderous task. Malcolm himself had been against the searches and displays of force in his own bodyguards and might easily have given the no-gun-search order that day. One policeman simply found Malcolm's security team to be a bunch of amateurs who were no match for paid killers: "I don't think he [Malcolm] was set up. I don't think they [the assassins] needed it."

According to writer Peter Goldman, who interviewed the New York City police extensively, the majority of the detectives on the case did feel that Malcolm had been betrayed by his own people— they just could not prove it. One of Malcolm's guards had been rumored to have taken cash in return for betraying him. However, when the police followed this lead, tracking the man to the South, he had disappeared. One detective said, "We figured this guy might be the man on the inside who ostensibly [outwardly] defected to Malcolm but really remained loyal to the Black Muslims. Where else did he get the money?" But with the suspect unavailable for questioning, the police had nothing concrete to go on. And in the final analysis, the New York City police had absolutely no proof to fit their contention that the murderer had cooperation from inside Malcolm's organization.

The police themselves were under suspicion from some quarters. Conspiracy theorists believe that although the New York City police clearly knew that Malcolm's life was in danger, they did little or nothing to prevent the assassination. Some theorists argue that the police, possibly acting in concert with the FBI or the U.S. government, were only too happy to see Malcolm die. In any case, the environment in which Malcolm X met his death was a violent one. Journalist Louis E. Lomax quoted in Michael Friedly's book blamed the racism and violence of American society for Malcolm's death as much as he blamed the gunmen: "This society, this violent and corrupt American society, this racist American society assassinated both Malcolm X and Martin Luther King, Jr. The men arrested may have pulled the trigger . . . but American society was . . . in concert with the assassins."

But it was Talmadge Hayer, Norman Butler, and Thomas Johnson who were in jail, awaiting trial for murdering Malcolm X.

3 The Trial and the Official Story: Did Malcolm's Murderers Act Alone?

On January 12, 1966, the trial of the men suspected of shooting Malcolm X began in New York City. The three defendants, Talmadge Hayer, Norman Butler, and Thomas Johnson, were charged with first-degree murder. Judge Charles Marks presided at the trial. Assistant District Attorney Vincent Dermody began the opening arguments against the three men.

The case against Hayer was the strongest, since he had actually been caught at the scene of the crime at the Audubon Ballroom, after being shot in the leg. The evidence against Butler and Johnson was considerably shakier. No hard physical evidence had been found to prove that they had been anywhere near the ballroom on the day that Malcolm X was assassinated. Although several witnesses testified that Butler and Johnson had been at the scene of the crime, most of these witnesses could identify either Butler or Johnson, but not both of them. This cast some doubt over the reliability of the witnesses' memories.

Hayer's lawyers defended him by arguing that Hayer had gone to the Audubon Ballroom only to see Malcolm X speak and not to shoot him. In testimony quoted by journalist Peter Goldman, who attended the trial, after the shooting, Hayer said he simply

> turned to see what was happening. And as I turned around, I could see some people moving—moving and standing, and as—then I heard a loud bang . . . I thought—I thought maybe it was an argument between some people and somebody had shot somebody in the argument. So I ducked on the floor, and I heard more shots, sound like it was coming from the direction of the stage. And when it stopped I started to get out of the ballroom. I ran for the exit. I fell a couple of times. I fell over somebody as I was

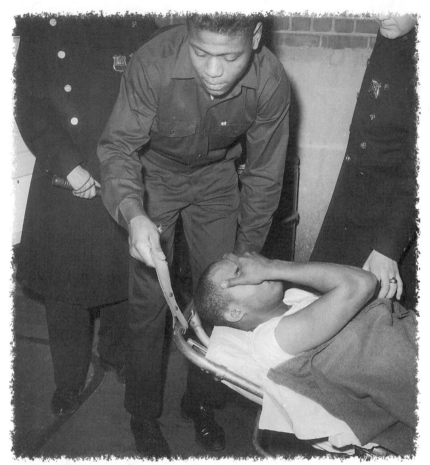

Suspect Talmadge Hayer is wheeled to a hospital after being wounded at the Audubon Ballroom. Hayer offered a weak defense during his trial for his part in the assassination.

running, and as I was going out of the ballroom my leg went numb—I think I was shot. . . . My leg caved in under me. I hopped. I hopped all the way out to the exit. . . . I slid down . . . and hit the bottom and fell on the floor . . . and I opened my eyes and I wasn't unconscious . . . so I crawled on my elbows and arms out the door. And when I went out the door a whole swab of people came out behind me, and they were kicking at me and grabbing at me, saying "Stop him, stop him, he killed—he killed Malcolm X. Stop him, stop him, he killed him, he killed him, he killed him."

Butler's defense was somewhat more convincing than Hayer's, but it also had holes in it. Butler's defense was that he had been

A Wife's Account

In this excerpt from trial testimony taken from the Goldman book, Betty Shabazz, the widow of Malcolm X, is testifying. She reports what she had seen when her husband was shot.

"There was chairs falling, people hollering . . . a succession of shots being fired. . . . My babies started crying, and they wanted to know if somebody was going to kill us . . . and I was trying to quiet them. Everyone had fallen to the floor, chairs were on the floor, people were crawling around, and I pushed them under a bench that had a back to it. . . . I covered the bench with my body, but one of them started crying [that] they couldn't breathe and they couldn't see, so I turned around to quiet them, and when I turned back around I saw people crawling on the floor, I saw folded chairs on the floor, and I saw someone gasp, like—you know—and I looked towards the stage. I didn't see my husband. . . . When I looked and didn't see him, I ran—started running to the stage—but they wouldn't let me go."

As Betty Shabazz exited the courtroom she stopped near the defense table and cried 'They killed my husband! They killed him!'"

Betty Shabazz (right) weeps outside the Audubon Ballroom after her husband was gunned down by assassins' bullets.

home, laid up with a bad leg at the time of the shooting. His doctor testified that Butler was incapacitated with an inflammation of the veins. "My leg was quite sore," Butler said. And his foot "was much too swollen for me to even put on my shoe correctly." When asked by Dermody if he had been in the Audubon Ballroom the day of the shooting, Butler said "emphatically no." When asked if he had run out of the ballroom after the shooting, Butler responded, "I couldn't run." But the weakness in Butler's alibi was that he had no witnesses to confirm it. No one had actually seen him at home during the time of the shooting.

Johnson's alibi was also weak. He claimed to have been at home with his wife and children the day that Malcolm X was shot. He claimed to have heard about the shooting from a neighbor. "Sometimes that afternoon—it was before dark, I don't remember the hour—Brother Edward came up. . . . He asked me did I hear the news. At the same time, he had a black portable radio in his hand, and that's when I found out that Malcolm had been killed." But Johnson's alibi was not particularly strong, as it rested on family members who, of course, would protect him. He also had a criminal past, with five convictions, and admitted to having a rifle in his home.

The defense team failed to present an alternative theory about what had happened at the Audubon Ballroom on the day of the crime. A stronger defense would have been to construct a theory that pointed a finger at other guilty parties rather than Hayer, Butler, and Johnson. However, the defense simply rested on trying to present alibis for the three men.

Although their alibis were weak, Butler and Johnson could not be that easily convicted because the prosecutor's case depended on a single witness, Cary Thomas. Thomas did describe the crime scene accurately. He was also able to correctly identify all three defendants as members of the Nation of Islam. Although this in and of itself was not a crime, if fit in neatly with the police theory that Malcolm X had been shot by paid assassins who were most probably Black Muslim enforcers. However, Cary Thomas's testimony was marred by his unsavory past and by his sometimes contradictory details.

At the trial Thomas said that he had sat in the nineteenth row of the audience. He saw Johnson sitting in a back booth. He saw Hayer stand up holding a pistol and yelling at Butler, "Man, what are you doing with your hand in my pocket?" Then Thomas heard a shot, he turned toward the podium and saw that "Hayer and Butler had [run] to the front . . . and they started shooting in the area of the stage where Malcolm X's body was laying. . . . The audience seemed to run and break, and everybody was running. . . . I crouched down behind a booth."

This version somewhat contradicted the story he had told previously to the grand jury. In his version to the grand jury, he said Butler and Johnson had reached the stage together; at the trial, he

Johnson was one of the men accused of shooting Malcolm X. His conviction depended on the testimony of one eyewitness.

Tales of a Bodyguard

This excerpt from the trial transcripts is taken from Peter Goldman's book, The Death and Life of Malcolm X. *At the trial, the defense examined Cary Thomas on his role at the Audubon Ballroom, where he was a bodyguard. But despite the defense's attempt to discredit him, Cary Thomas remained a star witness for the prosecution. Sabbatino asked*

"'. . . your own arms were free?'

'Yes, my arms were free.'

'Your hands were not tied?'

'Not tied.'

'Your legs were free?'

'Free.'

'And you still had a holster with a revolver?'

'Yes.'

'Did you do anything with these two men going toward
    Malcolm X?

Did you do anything with your gun to stop these two
    men?'

'No.'

'You were there as a member of the security guard to
    protect Malcolm X, weren't you?'

'Yes.'

'Or were you a fake protector?'

'I was just there.'

'Or were you part of any conspiracy?'

'I wasn't part of anything.'

'Against Malcolm X?'

'No, I wasn't.' "

---

claimed it was Johnson. Some details of identification were also muddled: Thomas originally claimed Hayer was a Muslim from a New York City mosque, then later identified him as being from a mosque in Jersey City. When cross-examined by the defense, Thomas said his sometimes contradictory testimony was because "I was quite upset and nervous and I could have made (a) mistake. . . . I had a fear for my life." However, in the end, Cary Thomas's testimony held up under cross-examination. It was his testimony that finally succeeded in convicting the three defendants.

A Confession

The most dramatic development came on February 28, about six weeks into the trial. Hayer told the judge and jury that he had lied in his earlier testimony and that now he wanted to tell the truth. Hayer confessed that he had committed the crime that he was accused of but that Butler and Johnson were not guilty. Hayer stated: "I just want the truth to be known that Butler and Johnson didn't have anything to do with this crime. I was there, I know what happened, I know the people that did take part in it, and they wasn't any of the people that had anything to do with it. I want the jury to know."

The prosecution cross-examined Hayer after his confession. The prosecution knew that Hayer was already guilty in the eyes of the jury, so they set out to prove that Hayer was simply trying to protect his Muslim coconspirators Butler and Johnson. Prosecutor Dermody asked, "Mr. Hayer—did somebody ask you and others to shoot and kill Malcolm X?" Hayer answered, "Well, yes, sir." The transcript of the trial excerpted in Peter Goldman's book showed that although Dermody probed further, Hayer was not giving away much information.

> Dermody: "When do you say you were first approached by anybody in connection with the assassination of Malcolm X?"
> Hayer: "Sometime in February, I guess . . . beginning of February."
> Dermody: "Who approached you?"
> Hayer: "I won't say."
> Dermody: "Where were you approached?"
> Hayer: "I won't say."

Hayer's testimony also included a version of the assassination that claimed four, rather than three, assassins were involved:

> Four people, two people sitting in the front row, man with the shotgun—short dark man with the beard—sitting around the fourth row from the front, man in the back; one man (in the back) starts commotion, says, "Get your hand out of my pocket," guards from the stage goes after this

man, man with the shotgun shoots Malcolm, two men on the front row shoot pistols.

Dermody asked Hayer, "And which of these men were you?" Hayer confessed, "One of the men sitting in the front row."

As the cross-examination continued, Dermody tried to pressure Hayer into confessing that the Black Muslims were involved and had even ordered the assassination, in keeping with the theory favored by the police. However, the trial transcriptions, again excerpted from Goldman, showed Hayer resisting this line of inquiry.

Dermody: "Let me ask you, Mr. Hayer, this person who approached you and the others to do this assassination—was this person, to your knowledge, a member of the Black Muslims?"
Hayer: "No, he was not."
Dermody: "Did this person tell you why he wanted to hire you and these others to assassinate Malcolm X?"
Hayer: "No, sir.". . .
Dermody: "What was your motive?"
Hayer: "Money."
Dermody: "Money?"
Hayer: "Mm-hm."
Dermody: "How much?"
Hayer: "I won't say."

That was the extent of the information that the prosecution was able to get out of Hayer. Hayer ultimately refused to name the person or persons who had hired him to assassinate Malcolm X and claimed that whoever had paid him was not from the Nation of Islam. Was Talmadge Hayer telling the truth? At that point in the trial, it was obvious to Hayer that the jury would convict him. Therefore, if he took responsibility for the crime he had nothing to lose—he was going to prison in any case. Hayer's attempts to clear his codefendants may have been motivated by a desire to get the other two men off. Or, Hayer may have been telling the truth or a partial version of what really had happened. He was still protecting the identity of whoever had ordered the assassination. Although Judge Charles Marks attempted to force Hayer to tell the jury who had hired him, Hayer resisted. The questions raised by Hayer's confession remained puzzling: Were Johnson and Butler

Under Cross-Examination

In another trial transcript taken from Goldman's book, Hayer is cross-examined by prosecutor Dermody. Hayer's confession in court did not negatively affect the prosecution's case.

"'Tell us how you were involved,' Dermody began.

'I had a weapon and I—'

'What kind of weapon did you have?'

'Forty-five.' . . .

'And did you fire that weapon at the deceased?'

'Yes, sir.'

'How many shots did you fire?'

'Maybe four.' . . .

'Did you fire right into his body?'

'I did.' . . .

'Give us the whole thing from the very beginning,' Dermody said.

'No, sir.'

'*What's that?*'

'No, sir.' . . .

'Let me ask you this question, Mr. Hayer—did somebody ask you and others to shoot and kill Malcolm X?'

'Well, yes, sir.'

'Do you know the name of that person who directed you to do it?'

'No, sir.'

'Well, did you receive orders or instructions from that person?'

'No, sir. No, sir.'

'You testified a few moments ago that you were told to do this by somebody, is that right?

You say you were offered some money?' Dermody pressed.

'Yes, sir.'

'To kill Malcolm X?'

'Yes, sir.'

'Did you ever *receive* any money for killing him?'

'No, sir.' . . .

'How much money were you offered to kill Malcolm X?'

'I don't care—can't say. I won't say.'"

Bullet holes are circled with chalk in the Audubon Ballroom after the slaying of Malcolm X. Although several people had been involved in the assassination, the police had a difficult time finding all of the perpetrators.

guilty or innocent? And if Hayer was a hired gun, then who hired him to kill Malcolm X?

Hayer was not the only one who claimed that Butler and Johnson were innocent. So did Benjamin Goodman, Malcolm's follower who had introduced him at the Audubon Ballroom just moments before the shooting. Goodman insisted that he knew both Butler and Johnson by sight, and that neither of them was present at the Audubon Ballroom. Both men were known Muslim enforcers, and presumably other members of Malcolm's security force would also have identified, and evicted, them.

Guilty as Charged

Unfortunately for Butler and Johnson, Talmadge Hayer's attempt to clear their names actually backfired. It looked to the jury as if Hayer was simply lying, particularly as he failed to implicate anyone else. The jury of twelve was composed of nine men and three women, some black and some white. Defense Attorney Sabbatino led off the closing argument for the defendants. His defense was rambling, almost incomprehensible. Despite the fact that Hayer had confessed, Sabbatino insisted, "This boy was not guilty of anything." He claimed that Hayer's confession was a "noble Christian act on his part" to get others off; this basically was an admission that Hayer had lied.

The jury was none too impressed by these closing defense arguments. In contrast, Vincent Dermody, the prosecuting attorney, gave a clear final speech. In it, he emphasized the Black Muslim connections to the defendants and their guilt:

> We do not claim, we don't say we intend to prove or can prove . . . that Elijah Muhammad . . . had ordered the death of Malcolm X and designated these three defendants to be the killers. . . . [However] I submit that these three defendants are members of the Black Muslim organization. And the evidence definitely indicates that these three defendants caused his death. . . . Ordinarily, if a person makes up his mind to kill somebody, he does it in secret. He doesn't want any witnesses available. It's done in the dead of night, secretly, quietly. But when you consider the evidence . . . whoever did it chose to do it in the presence of between 200 and 400 people in broad daylight in a public room. . . . Is it abusing your common sense to suggest that it was done deliberately in the presence of these people as an object lesson to Malcolm's followers that this is what can happen and what will happen?

The jury was out for twenty hours and twenty minutes. On March 10, 1966, the jury's foreman read out the verdicts. The verdict on Talmadge Hayer: guilty. Norman Butler, guilty. Thomas Johnson, guilty. The jury declared all three men guilty of murder in the first degree.

The men were automatically sentenced to life in prison. Each was eligible for parole after twenty-seven years. Sabbatino, for the defense, predicted, "I don't think you have a solution here that history will support." He could not have known quite how true his words were. Hayer and Johnson and Butler went first to Sing Sing State Prison and then to an upstate New York prison. However, although the jury was convinced of their guilt, the world at large was not convinced that the killers of Malcolm X had been found.

Who killed Malcolm X? Was it the three men who now sat in prison? Or were the unanswered questions about the case pointing to other assassins?

4 Did the Nation of Islam Order Malcolm X Killed?

Although the three men accused of the murder of Malcolm X had been sentenced to life imprisonment, the trial raised more questions than it answered, the most important of which was whether the Black Muslims had actually ordered the assassination. The Black Muslims certainly appeared to have a motive to kill Malcolm X: He had deserted Elijah Muhammad along with Muhammad's Black Muslim principles and beliefs. Malcolm X was now competing for converts for his own newly formed organization and drawing members away from the Nation of Islam.

Did Elijah Muhammad himself order the execution of the man who had been like a son to him? Because Malcolm had worked so closely with Muhammad, he was privy to some damning information about the leader. For example, not only did Malcolm know that Muhammad had fathered several illegitimate children, he also knew that funds had been mismanaged, even embezzled, from the treasury of the Nation of Islam. Evidence of this corruption was given in 1990 by Benjamin Goodman, a follower of Malcolm's who had also been in the Nation of Islam. Michael Friedly quotes Goodman: "There was a lot of money floating around and a lot of people were spending money in areas where it shouldn't be spent."

Malcolm had even begun to publicly attack the Nation of Islam for corruption. He said that the national secretary of the Nation of Islam was running the organization for one purpose: to get all the money out of it that he possibly could. Goodman recalls that Malcolm X "began to speak out against some of the expenses of the family members who were buying fur coats, spending a lot of money in nightclubs, wearing diamonds and other expensive jewelry—from donated money, not earned." In conclusion, Goodman says that Malcolm X threatened high-up Muslim officials' "access to money and living well."

Elijah Muhammad publicly denied any involvement in the killing. However, the Nation of Islam was most probably responsible for the firebombing of Malcolm's house just days before his death. The firebombing reflected not only the Nation of Islam's anger toward Malcolm and a disregard for his family's safety, but also their willingness to use force and even murder to gain their ends. In conversations with friends, Malcolm X hinted in his last days that the Nation of Islam was after him. Anonymous callers attempted to frighten and harass him. Malcolm began keeping a loaded automatic rifle handy at all times. He was sure the Muslims would eventually kill him.

The Nation of Islam had the motive to kill Malcolm; it also had the will to kill. The Fruit of Islam, in particular, was becoming renowned for acts of violence. In a quote taken from Michael

"To Put a Bullet into Me"

In his Autobiography, *Malcolm X spoke directly about threats the Black Muslims had made against his life.*

"The first direct order for my death was issued through a Mosque Seven official who previously had been a close assistant. Another previously close assistant of mine was assigned to do the job. He was a brother with a knowledge of demolition; he was asked to wire my car to explode when I turned the ignition key. But this brother, it happened, had seen too much of my total loyalty to carry out his order. Instead, he came to me. I thanked him for my life. I told him what was really going on. . . . He was stunned almost beyond belief.

This brother was close to others in the Mosque Seven circle who might subsequently be called upon to eliminate me. He said he would take it upon himself to enlighten each of them enough so that they wouldn't allow themselves to be used.

This first direct death-order was how, finally, I began to arrive at my psychological divorce from the Nation of Islam.

I began to see, wherever I went—on the streets, in business places, on elevators, sidewalks, in passing cars—the faces of Muslims whom I knew, and I knew that any of them might be waiting to try and put a bullet into me."

Friedly's book, Wallace D. Muhammad, the son of Elijah Muhammad, who had also eventually become disillusioned with his father's organization, said of the Fruit of Islam:

> It became a political order, and it was hooligans; it became nothing but a hooligan outfit, a hoodlum outfit, of men who were just playing politics and playing revolution. Not a revolution that carried its attack outside; a revolution that kept its attack inside. Directed at leaders who showed a future. That showed promise that maybe they would become the leader. And directed at well-meaning, innocent people in the community.

A Family's Suspicion

In the ten years following Malcolm X's death, little new information was divulged about the case. In 1975 Elijah Muhammad died of natural causes. His son, Wallace, led the Nation of Islam into a more moderate phase. Elijah Muhammad's death and the less militant stance by the Nation made it possible for more information to come to light on the assassination of Malcolm X, as people were less afraid to speak out.

Betty Shabazz, Malcolm's widow, had long maintained privately that the Black Muslims had killed her husband and that the order had come from high up in the Nation's hierarchy. She blamed in particular Louis Farrakhan, who had been known as Louis X when he was a minister in the Nation of Islam. Betty Shabazz even stated the accusation publicly on NBC television in 1985.

Louis Farrakhan had been the national minister in the Nation of Islam, a position once held by Malcolm X. When Malcolm left the Black Muslims, Farrakhan loudly and publicly attacked him. Farrakhan admitted that the Black Muslims had feelings of envy toward Malcolm: "As we began to grow, jealousy arose in the ranks against Malcolm. . . . As Malcolm began to evolve and to grow, this jealousy would intensify." In the Nation of Islam's newspaper, *Muhammad Speaks*, Farrakhan called Malcolm "the chief hypocrite" for leaving the Nation of Islam and its leader, Elijah Muhammad. Farrakhan had even said that Malcolm was "worthy of death."

After the shooting of Malcolm X, many people believed that Louis Farrakhan was the man behind the assassins and that he had

Wallace D. Muhammad, son of Elijah Muhammad, believed that his father's organization was responsible for the assassination of Malcolm X.

ordered the shooting. Farrakhan had certainly encouraged violent actions against Malcolm with his rhetoric. After the assassination, his words would come back to haunt him and tarnish his reputation even after he left the Nation of Islam and formed his own organization, in a move similar to Malcolm's. Farrakhan went on to some success in the African-American community in his efforts to decrease drug abuse and violence among youth. Still he was blamed for the shooting of Malcolm X, particularly by members of Malcolm's own family.

Farrakhan vigorously denied his involvement in the assassination. He said that the charge was used to discredit him as a rising African-American leader: "Now to take Malcolm as a hero of the Black struggle and in some way attempt to make Louis Farrakhan guilty for Malcolm's assassination is really a blow that is not just low, it strikes you at the ankles if someone is shooting for your stomach. That is as low as you can get."

One of the newest and best-researched books on the shooting, Michael Friedly's *Malcolm X: The Assassination*, points a decided finger at Louis Farrakhan. Author Friedly says:

> Farrakhan helped create the climate of hatred that finally killed Malcolm X. His editorials were the most direct attacks that were printed in the Nation's newspapers during this time, and his prediction that "the die is set, and Malcolm shall not escape" helped convince the Muslims that Malcolm X should be killed. The assassination of Malcolm X was not a simple act of violence that was conceived and executed within a matter of seconds. Rather, it was a complicated process of establishing an environment that was ripe for murder. First, the members of the Nation of Islam had to believe that Malcolm was "worthy of death" as

Long before the assassination, Louis Farrakhan preached that Malcolm X should be ostracized and condemned by the Nation of Islam.

Farrakhan wrote in *Muhammad Speaks*. Second, individual members of the Nation of Islam had to be convinced to actually carry out the execution. The final step, of course, was the actual assassination. While Farrakhan almost certainly played little or no role in the actual planning of the assassination, he was instrumental in providing the context for the murder.

A New Confession

Only after ten years had passed following the death of Malcolm X was dramatic information revealed. In 1977, three years after Elijah Muhammad had died, Talmadge Hayer gave a new confession. Hayer wrote out his confession in a three-page affidavit: "I am writing this affidavit in the hope that it will clear my co-defendants of the charges brought against them in this case." In the confession Hayer told yet another version of the shooting in the Audubon Ballroom. Hayer admitted that he had lied at the trial, both in his initial testimony and then in his so-called confession which contradicted it. The first lie was when he claimed he was innocent of shooting Malcolm X. The second lie came when he was trying to clear Butler and Johnson and said that the Black Muslims were not involved in the assassination.

In 1977 Hayer admitted that he was both guilty of the crime and that the Black Muslims had indeed been involved in the assassination of Malcolm X. Elijah Muhammad was dead, and Hayer was no longer trying to protect the Nation of Islam. He explained his motive for the assassination:

> I thought it was very bad for anyone to go against the teachings of the Hon. Elijah, then known as the last messenger of God. I was told that Muslims should more or less be willing to fight against hypocrites and I agreed [with] that. There was no money paid to me for my part in this. I thought I was fighting for truth and right.

In a second affidavit, written in 1978 a few months after the first, Hayer attempted to clear up some of the inconsistencies in the trial version of the shooting of Malcolm X. The purpose of the second statement, Hayer wrote, was to "clear up any doubt as to what took place in the killing of Malcolm X and the [innocence] of Norman Butler and Thomas Johnson."

Chaos in the Ballroom

After his prison confession, Talmadge Hayer gave an account quoted in Malcolm X: The Assassination, *of how he was captured that day in the Audubon Ballroom. To Hayer, as to many eyewitnesses, the scene was one of extreme confusion. He remembers:*

"There was a lot of commotion and stuff. . . . I remember though—there was quite a few guns in that place being fired. I didn't even know I got shot in the left leg. Even to today I think I got shot in my right. Because there was this guy shooting at my right side. I didn't see how I got shot on my left side. . . . I was just trying to make a commotion, man, I fired off a couple of shots. . . . There was one person, he was running in front of me. I think it was Leon. He came out before I did, because I was shot in my leg so I couldn't move fast. I was only trying to get outside. He was the only one [of the assassins] I could say went out before I did. Other people [accomplices] I couldn't see. They must have been after [behind] me. There was one guy I think he said I shot in the foot or something like this here. For the most part, I was just trying to get out. And I was hit in the leg. I didn't see the guy that shot me, you know. So I just hopped, man. I was hopping with one leg, and I slid down the banister, fell on the ground and—I don't know. And don't ask me why and how—there was an officer out there. And it was fortunate, because my life was spared [from being killed by the crowd]."

Hayer reconstructed the scene of the crime. He explained how the assassination had been planned and how two older Black Muslims had asked him to join their plot to kill Malcolm X. Hayer said the assassins had parked a few blocks from the ballroom and then prepared to shoot Malcolm. He said he had been sitting in the front of the auditorium, with the .45 automatic. This matched the eyewitness accounts of Hayer shooting at Malcolm X's dying body.

Hayer's new confession did clear up some puzzling problems in the case, but it left one large question unanswered. Who had given the order to shoot Malcolm X? Hayer said he did not know if anyone high up in the Nation of Islam had given a direct order to assassinate Malcolm. Hayer told attorney William Kunstler that a total of four men were involved in the plot and that all four were members of the Nation of Islam from the Newark, New Jersey, mosque. However, Hayer never pointed a finger at Louis Farrakhan, Elijah Muhammad, or any other major Black Muslim figure.

Hayer's prison confession cast increasing doubt on the extent of Johnson's and Butler's involvement in the assassination. But guilty or innocent, the two men were still paying for their alleged crime in prison.

A New View of the Assassination

Talmadge Hayer's confession had enough new information in it for historians to paint a different picture of the assassination than the one that had come out at the trial. Michael Friedly, in his 1992 book, *Malcolm X: The Assassination*, created the most up-to-date account of the shooting of Malcolm X. Using Hayer's confession, author Friedly was able to reconstruct the following version of events.

According to Friedly, a total of five gunmen in overcoats that covered their weapons slipped by Malcolm X's security in the Audubon Ballroom. They had no trouble getting past security, because Malcolm had told his guards not to search anyone coming into the ballroom. Also, Malcolm's security was looking only for members of the paramilitary Fruit of Islam from New York. Talmadge Hayer was from Newark and knew that although there was a slight possibility he would be recognized, it was unlikely as "I was (from) out of town, for one thing. The other people that I was with, they was from out of town. Even though there was a few people now in Malcolm's organization that was also from Jersey. I don't know exactly how many. I don't recall seeing any of them." Hayer's account explains that although Malcolm's security was not as tight as it might have been, Malcolm's own men were actually not directly implicated in letting the assassins in, as the New York City police had originally suspected.

The presence of five gunmen clarified a point of confusion left over from the trial—although only three gunmen were tried for the crime, the police had theorized that another two or three were present in the ballroom. Neither Butler nor Johnson was involved according to Hayer. Rather, Hayer and a Black Muslim named Leon sat in the front row, on the left side facing the stage. Here again was a clarification, for although the prosecution had placed Hayer in the crime scene to the right of the stage, eyewitnesses had actually seen him on the left. Hayer carried the .45 pistol, while Leon concealed the Luger. Behind them sat another assassin, identified by Hayer as William X, who held a hidden sawed-off shotgun.

Two other members of the assassination team were in the ballroom. Both of them were unarmed and were there to make sure that all went well for the gunmen. After the shooting it would be easy for the unarmed men to simply mingle with the crowd and slip away unnoticed. A man identified by Hayer as Brother Wilbur was to cause the initial disturbance to focus attention away from Hayer, Leon, and William. The fifth man, named Ben, sat in the second row to anticipate problems. It was Wilbur who shouted "Man, get your hands out of my pocket." Then William opened his overcoat and opened fire on Malcolm. Hayer and Leon also fired directly into Malcolm's body.

Wilbur and Ben disappeared into the confusion of the crowd. William dropped his weapon and ran. Leon also fled. It was only Talmadge Hayer who was shot in the leg, trapped by the crowd, and arrested by the police. According to Hayer, of all the assassins, he was the only one to stand trial. And of the three men convicted of the shooting of Malcolm X, he was the only one who was guilty.

More Unresolved Questions

The prison confession of Talmadge Hayer shed light on the actual scene in the Audubon Ballroom. It identified all five assassins in logical locations throughout the ballroom. It also explained that although Malcolm X's security was lax and the New York City police were not present, these factors only made the assassination easier; they did not cause it. In addition, Hayer provided the motive for the five Black Muslims who killed Malcolm X: loyalty to Elijah Muhammad. The assassins apparently wanted to protect Elijah Muhammad because they believed that Malcolm X knew secrets that could be used to discredit the leader of the Nation of Islam.

The assassins were influenced by the rhetoric directed at Malcolm from the Nation of Islam. Hayer remembered: "The talk [then] was real heavy coming from the ministers at that time, man. Because I'll tell you the truth, man, I felt that it was really putting the FOI [Fruit of Islam] to a test, y'know. And it was never in most cases said directly, but it was like a seed planting." And there was one Black Muslim leader who indeed said directly: "Only those who wish to be led to hell, or their doom, will follow Malcolm. The die is set, and Malcolm shall not escape. . . ." The speaker of these inflammatory words, of course, was Louis Farrakhan.

By 1981 some of the facts that cast doubt on the trial were already public knowledge. On *60 Minutes*, television journalist Mike Wallace reported nationally that Butler and Johnson might have been falsely accused of murder. Witnesses came forward to say that they had lied when they had accused the two men. Michael

Elijah Muhammad denied any connection with the slaying of Malcolm X. Muhammad claimed that Malcolm was a victim of his own teachings. It remains a mystery as to whether Muhammad was directly involved.

Friedly published his account of the assassination in 1992. But of course the missing four men were never found, nor could they be, after so many years had elapsed. And Butler and Johnson were never freed. Thus, although Talmadge Hayer's prison confession changed some of the details of the trial theory, including, importantly, the innocence of two convicted men, it did not challenge the basic idea that the Black Muslims had killed Malcolm X.

However, one basic question remained. Were the gunmen really working alone, or was there a leader who had given the order to pull the trigger?

5 CIA, FBI, and a Daughter's Revenge

As in the assassination of John F. Kennedy, new theories continue to be offered to explain the assassination of Malcolm X. These less-documented theories about Malcolm X's death are included here because each reflects beliefs about his life and death. Malcolm at times seemed unconvinced that the Black Muslims were trying to kill him. His words to writer Alex Haley cast some doubt about who Malcolm thought his enemies were:

> The more I keep thinking about this thing, the things that have been happening lately, I'm not at all sure that it's the Muslims. I know what they can do, and what they can't, and they can't do some of the stuff recently going on. Now, I'm going to tell you, the more I keep thinking about what happened to me in France, I think I'm going to quit saying it's the Muslims.

The CIA Theory

What did happen to Malcolm X in France? On February 9 of the year he was killed, the French government denied Malcolm X entry to France. Malcolm, as well as some conspiracy theorists, believe that the Central Intelligence Agency (CIA) pressured the French government into refusing him or that the French government knew that the CIA was planning to murder him and did not want him killed on French soil. According to this theory, the CIA was antagonistic toward Malcolm because he was becoming increasingly involved in global politics and was visiting the emerging socialist nations of Africa as well as Fidel Castro's Cuba. The theory reasons that because Malcolm X was a leader of African Americans, he might actually present a threat to the U.S. government if he became a socialist revolutionary.

The belief that the CIA had a hand in assassinating Malcolm X stems from remarks that Malcolm made. After his death they were repeated and published. Some observers believed that the CIA was implicated, even if indirectly, in Malcolm's death. Paul Lee, a Malcolm X scholar, stated, "I don't believe that the Nation of Islam alone could have pulled off the assassination that day." He believes that although the Black Muslims actually shot Malcolm, the assassins were paid by the CIA.

Theories surrounding the death of Malcolm X continue to surface and are fueled by recent books and movies. Was the CIA involved in the assassination?

Malcolm with spiritual leaders in Cairo. Malcolm believed that the CIA tried to poison his food while he was visiting the country.

Peter Goldman, a journalist who followed Malcolm X's career closely, and who wrote the first important book on Malcolm called *The Death and Life of Malcolm X*, does not believe that the French government was acting in conjunction with the CIA. Goldman proposes that the French government was acting on its own behalf, for the French did not want Malcolm X to incite African students living in Paris. The French were particularly sensitive to African liberation at this time because two of their newly freed colonies, Senegal and the Ivory Coast, were trying to protect moderate governments from radicalism.

In addition to being barred from France, Malcolm X also blamed the CIA for another incident during his foreign travels. Toward the end of his life, when he was visiting Egypt, Malcolm became violently ill. On July 23, 1964, Malcolm ate dinner at Cairo's Hilton Hotel. He fell violently ill in the middle of the night and was taken to the hospital, where his stomach was pumped. Malcolm believed he had been poisoned by the CIA and told his half-sister, Ella, "that the CIA was definitely responsible for it." Here again, Peter Goldman does not buy the CIA theory. He proposes that the incident in Egypt was no incident at all, just a simple case of food poisoning or a stomach ailment.

Although the CIA theory seems shaky at best, it remains appealing. However, implicating the CIA in Malcolm's death is more the work of paranoia than of historical accuracy. Eleven years after

Malcolm X's death, the CIA stated that the agency had never had anything to do with Malcolm's organization.

The FBI Theory

Unlike the CIA, the Federal Bureau of Investigation's (FBI) links to Malcolm X are a proven fact. Indeed, the FBI began following what Malcolm X was doing soon after he came out of prison and became active in the Nation of Islam. The FBI opened its file in 1953 and continued to keep close tabs on him until his death in 1965.

Why was the FBI interested in Malcolm X? A 1968 FBI memorandum tells part of the story when it states that some of the long-range goals of the bureau include actions to "prevent the coalition of militant black nationalist groups" because "an effective coalition of black nationalist groups might be the first step toward . . . a true black revolution." The memorandum goes on to state that the FBI must prevent "the rise of a 'messiah' who could unify and electrify . . . the black militant nationalist movement. Malcolm X might have been such a 'messiah.'"

The theory that links the FBI to the assassination of Malcolm X does not implicate the FBI in the shooting but exposes the fact that they might have prevented it but failed to do so. The FBI was following Malcolm at the time of the shooting. There are tape-recorded conversations between Malcolm and FBI agents who came to his home. Agents even went so far as to try to buy the names of Nation of Islam members from Malcolm and the bureau tapped his phones. At the time of his death, the FBI was as close to Malcolm as members of his own family. And yet the FBI failed to protect Malcolm in the last months of his life. Radical lawyer William Kunstler sums up the situation by saying that although the FBI was not directly involved in the slaying of Malcolm X, "They created the atmosphere where it could occur."

The FBI file on Malcolm X is now a matter of public record. In fact, it is available in book form, all 422 pages, collected in *Malcolm X: The FBI File* by Clayborne Carson. In February 1965, a few weeks before he was shot, the FBI recorded an interview with Malcolm X on Chicago television. In the discussion, Malcolm said directly that there had already been attacks on his life because he had left the Nation of Islam. The FBI also investigated the firebombing and destruction of Malcolm's house, and had first-hand knowledge of the threat to his life. Had the FBI considered

Malcolm X a reputable public figure, the bureau would no doubt have taken many steps to protect him. But because the FBI saw Malcolm as a revolutionary leader of African Americans and a potential threat to the peace and security of the nation, the bureau was interested in keeping him under surveillance, rather than protecting him. As the FBI took no steps to protect Malcolm X, the bureau perhaps contributed, through negligence, to his death.

The first page in the FBI file on Malcolm X. Some believe that the fact that the FBI did not protect Malcolm X from assassination implicates the organization in his death.

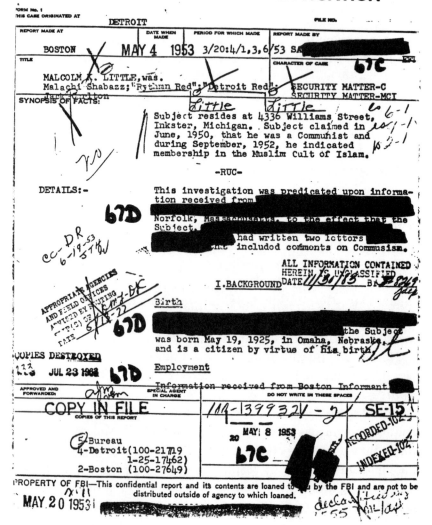

An Alternative Assassination Theory

There were other theories about who had killed Malcolm X. James Farmer, the founder of the influential Congress of Racial Equality (CORE) believed that Malcolm had been killed by drug lords. Farmer started out by saying that the assassination was "a political killing with international implications." The *New York Times* correctly interpreted this to mean that Farmer thought that Malcolm X had been killed for preaching against drug use in the Black community. Farmer's views were apparently confirmed when Percy Sutton, Malcolm X's lawyer, told him: "Jim, I don't know whether you realize how right you were in what you said about Malcolm's murder. Furthermore, I understand the smart boys in Harlem are wondering how you could know so much from the outside."

Farmer's theory is discussed in Michael Friedly's book *Malcolm X: The Assassination*. It is included as an interesting theory by a reputable source. However, Friedly finally concludes that "Farmer presents an interesting hypothesis, but his allegations must be dismissed in the face of far more plausible explanations of why Malcolm X was murdered."

A Daughter's Revenge

Thirty years after the assassination of Malcolm X, the generally accepted theory of his death was that he had been shot by Black Muslims. Historians had debunked the idea that the CIA was implicated, but full reports showed that the FBI was aware of the threat to Malcolm's life and did nothing. The major remaining question in the case was whether a specific leader in the Nation of Islam had given the order to assassinate Malcolm X and whether the Nation or such individuals would ever take public responsibility for the act.

Although the case was no longer in the public limelight, Malcolm's family continued to suffer from his loss. His twin daughters were born after his death, leaving a total of six children fatherless. The three oldest girls had actually seen their father shot in the Audubon Ballroom. It was Malcolm and Betty's second daughter, Qubilah Shabazz, who seemed the most negatively affected by her father's death and who would try to take revenge.

Betty Shabazz made no secret of the fact that she believed that Louis Farrakhan was responsible for the death of Malcolm X. This belief was inherited by Qubilah. On Thursday, January 12, 1995, Qubilah Bahiya Shabazz, thirty-four, was arrested in Minneapolis on federal charges of trying to hire a hit man to kill Louis Farrakhan. Once again, the assassination of Malcolm X was in the news.

Qubilah Shabazz was not working on her own. In fact, a government informant named Michael Fitzpatrick played an important part in the so-called plot to kill Louis Farrakhan. Michael Fitzpatrick had been a government informant for some time. He was also an old friend of Qubilah Shabazz's. However, she had not heard from him in fourteen years. Then, on Memorial Day of 1994 he suddenly called her on the telephone.

The FBI recorded at least forty calls between Michael Fitzpatrick and Qubilah Shabazz. The transcriptions of the telephone calls filled 312 pages. Of the forty calls, Michael Fitzpatrick made thirty-eight between July and November 1994. He also did most of the talking, as Shabazz spoke only occasionally.

Michael Fitzpatrick was facing a drug charge in Minneapolis and perhaps hoped to lessen the penalty by working for the FBI. In the telephone calls Fitzpatrick talked about Louis Farrakhan as the murderer of Shabazz's father. He then tried to talk Qubilah into a plot to kill Farrakhan.

Reports in the *New York Times* said that the transcripts made it clear that Qubilah Shabazz hated and feared Louis Farrakhan. She also held him directly responsible for her father's death. But the transcripts also showed that although Shabazz might want Farrakhan dead, she was not all that committed to actually killing him. The transcripts show her wavering:

> "I thought you wanted to be involved," Fitzpatrick said. "I mean I would still be willing to do this [kill Farrakhan] but now with you—"
> "Being iffy," interrupted Shabazz.
> "Yeah, iffy is one."
> "Unreliable?" she asked.

If Shabazz was being unreliable it was because she was indeed having second thoughts about murdering Farrakhan, even though she held him directly responsible for her father's death. By November 1994 Shabazz told Fitzpatrick that she was now too worried about their plan to execute it and wanted to postpone it. She asked him a blunt question about one of her fears, but he answered with a lie:

> "Are you an informant?" Shabazz wanted to know.
> "Am I an informant?" echoed Michael Fitzpatrick.
> "Yeah."
> "Quibilah, please," he said. "No. I'm not an informant."

Settlement Instead of Trial

On the basis of these taped conversations, federal charges were brought against Qubilah Shabazz. She pleaded not guilty, and was released on bail. If convicted, Shabazz was facing a $2.25 million fine as well as up to ninety years in prison. Her lawyers were Percy Sutton and William Kunstler, who was famous for his defense of liberal and radical causes.

Shabazz's family, and the African-American community at large, rallied around Qubilah Shabazz. Many admired her as the daughter

Qubilah Shabazz, Malcolm's daughter, after being charged with trying to hire a hit man to murder Louis Farrakhan. The Shabazz family believes that Farrakhan was responsible for the assassination.

of Malcolm X, while close friends knew she was an emotionally fragile young woman. In an unpredictable move, Louis Farrakhan reacted in a sympathetic and supportive manner. Farrakhan had publicly declared Malcolm X "worthy of death." And he had just as publicly been accused of aiding in the murder of Malcolm X. Now, Louis Farrakhan said simply that his "heart goes out to the Shabazz family." This was the first gesture he would make in what would prove to be the final chapter in the debate on who murdered Malcolm X.

On May 1, 1995, just as the trial was about to begin, Qubilah Shabazz avoided having to stand trial by agreeing to accept responsibility for her vague attempts to take the life of Louis Farrakhan. Federal district court judge James Rosenbaum quickly

A Taped Conversation

Don Terry, in a special report to the New York Times, *recounted conversations that had been taped between Qubilah Shabazz and Michael Fitzpatrick.*

" 'You can definitely do it without getting caught, right?' she asked Mr. Fitzpatrick.

'There are no definites in this,' he replied. 'The only way to get caught, is like I said, if there's a police informant, which you're not, I'm not—which you know—you brought it to me, you know who I am. And the second one is the cops stumbling on you. Other than that, you want to know the truth, if things are set up right, there's really no way to get caught.'

'Hm,' she sighed.

'What?' he asked.

'I'm just grateful,' she said.

'Don't be grateful yet, hon,' he said. 'You know, right now it's all [expletive] talk, you know what I mean? We'll let the—actions speak for themselves.'

A few moments later, he said: 'I'm glad that you came to me with this. Then, you said you just went to one person with it, and then, you came to me. I'm sure you would have gone to someone else down the road or you would have done it yourself. I'm glad you didn't, you know, I'm glad you're not going to jail.' "

Louis Farrakhan, the man Qubilah Shabazz may have attempted to have killed in revenge for the death of her father. Shabazz came under FBI investigation for the plot.

agreed to approve the solution reached by the prosecutors and Shabazz's defense. He put her on two-year probation, ordered her to spend three months in a psychiatric, drug, and alcohol treatment program, and instructed her to get a job. "I just want to get on with my life," Shabazz said after the hearing. "I want to live it privately."

The case of Qubilah Shabazz reopened the assassination of Malcolm X in the public eye. The FBI was still monitoring members of Malcolm's family, just as it had monitored him up until the time of his death. As Clayborne Carson, the author of *Malcolm X: The FBI File* wrote:

The FBI's interest in Malcolm did not end with his death. Instead, the Bureau's efforts to combat the new forms of racial militancy became more ruthless in the post-Malcolm era. Aware of the threat that Malcolm might have posed if he had succeeded in unifying the black militant community, the FBI attempted to exacerbate [intensify] conflicts among the various factions that identified themselves with Malcolm's ideas.

However, in attempting to frame Malcolm X's daughter, the FBI had an unsympathetic case. Public opinion was with Shabazz, particularly as the transcripts of the telephone calls gave the impression that Michael Fitzpatrick had led Shabazz on and suggested the plot to her. It appeared, too, that Shabazz may have hoped to marry Fitzpatrick. The case looked like entrapment. Fitzpatrick even admitted that he had been promised a fee of forty-five thousand dollars by the U.S. government to record his phone calls with Shabazz and to then testify at her trial.

However, the FBI's attempts to entrap Malcolm's daughter did not prove that the agency assassinated Malcolm X. Rather, it

Qubilah Shabazz and her mother talk to reporters after Qubilah is acquitted of attempting to hire a hit man to kill Farrakhan.

showed that the FBI was still antagonistic toward Malcolm's family and had probably done nothing to prevent his murder. Qubilah Shabazz signed an agreement accepting responsibility for her involvement in the plot to kill Farrakhan. However, upon leaving the courtroom, Shabazz immediately contradicted the statement. She said she had been coerced into signing, and that the statement was not true, but she was quoted in the *New York Times* as saying that signing it was "better than being incarcerated." But whether or not Qubilah Shabazz accepted responsibility, there was an unexpected by-product of the FBI's prosecution of Malcolm X's daughter. This was to bring the Shabazz family and Louis Farrakhan into direct contact thirty years after Malcolm's death. This new meeting between former enemies was to heal old wounds and the feelings of an entire community. It would also shed additional light on the murder of Malcolm X and perhaps provide the last missing piece to the puzzle of who had ordered his assassination.

EPILOGUE

The Nation of Islam Confesses—But Not Completely

Harlem never expected to see hundreds of people fill its Apollo Theater to witness a meeting between Louis Farrakhan and Betty Shabazz. But Shabazz and Farrakhan had been brought together by the arrest of Qubilah Shabazz. Despite the fact that he was the intended victim of a vague plot hatched between Qubilah and the informant Michael Fitzpatrick, Farrakhan had shown immediate public support for the Shabazz family.

At the meeting at the Apollo Theater, in the same neighborhood where Malcolm X had been shot thirty years before, Louis Farrakhan finally admitted that Malcolm had been killed by the Nation of Islam. He said: "Members of the Nation of Islam were involved in the assassination of Malcolm. We cannot deny our part." But he went on: "But we cannot let the real culprit get away with dividing us. The Government of the United States is the outside force that divided us."

Farrakhan's statement at the meeting in Harlem was momentous. Some observers took a cynical look at Farrakhan's attitude, speculating that as Malcolm X had become a symbol of the African-American community, it would do Farrakhan some good to be allied with the Shabazz family. Also, the suspicion that Farrakhan was implicated in Malcolm X's death had tarnished his reputation for years.

At the Apollo Theater, Louis Farrakhan denied that he had had any direct involvement in the slaying of Malcolm X. His statement implicated the Nation of Islam but left it unclear whether he was simply admitting that the assassins were in the Nation or whether an order had come from above. However, the mood at the Apollo was one of reconciliation. The last speaker of the evening was Dr. Betty Shabazz, who gratefully thanked Louis Farrakhan for his support of her daughter.

Reporters watching the public reconciliation were divided on how genuine it was. Some thought that Shabazz was simply protecting her daughter. Congressman Charles B. Rangel, the U.S. representative from Manhattan proposed a different theory: Both Farrakhan and Shabazz made a show of peace to prevent any possible reprisals against the Shabazz family, presumably from supporters of Louis Farrakhan. But Congressman Rangel added that it was all for the good, whatever the motive: "Who cares whether Rabin loves Arafat? Who cares whether Nelson Mandela really likes his jailers well enough to have them to his inauguration? It's not what is in their hearts that counts. It's whether they are both working towards peace."

Who Killed Malcolm X?

Thirty years after the murder of Malcolm X, the fact is that Malcolm was shot by members of the Nation of Islam. Louis Farrakhan and others within the Nation contributed to an atmosphere of hate and violence that led to the shooting. The prison confession of one of the convicted assassins and Louis Farrakhan's statements at the Apollo Theater all bear this out.

There are still unanswered questions in the case, questions that the passage of time makes less and less likely to be answered. The basic questions remain: Who gave the order to shoot Malcolm?

Louis Farrakhan and Betty Shabazz meet at the Apollo Theater, where Farrakhan denied direct involvement in the assassination.

Long after death, the message of charismatic leader Malcolm X remains an inspiration for many people around the world.

and Were innocent men tried and imprisoned while guilty men went free?

Malcolm X is remembered today as a charismatic speaker and leader. He was a man who always believed in self-determination for African Americans in the United States. When Betty Shabazz spoke at the Apollo Theater on that May evening in 1995, she spoke of the legacy her husband had left behind and recounted the fact that Malcolm had foreseen his own death. But even though

Malcolm X had predicted his own assassination, he had told his wife: "Don't be bitter."

These were words of peace from a man who had often spoken of violence and who had died violently. They were words to help heal a family and a community: "Don't be bitter."

For Further Reading

Roger Barr, *The Importance of Malcolm X.* San Diego: Lucent Books, 1994. A thorough account of Malcolm X's life, philosophies, goals, and legacy. Geared toward young adults, this book includes many pictures and a timeline.

William Dudley, ed., *The Civil Rights Movement: Opposing Viewpoints.* San Diego: Greenhaven Press, 1996. This anthology includes authors of varied and contrasting opinions, including Malcolm X and Martin Luther King Jr., presenting readers with arguments of different positions on the Civil Rights Movement.

Nikki Grimes, *Malcolm X: A Force for Change.* New York: Fawcett Columbine, 1992. Targeted for middle-school readers, this volume covers Malcolm's entire life; the controversy surrounding his assassination is only briefly addressed, however.

Patricia and Frederick McKissack, *The Civil Rights Movement in America from 1865 to the Present.* Chicago: Childrens Press, 1987. This well-illustrated text covers Black American history after the Civil War. Includes the contributions of whites as well as blacks to the civil rights movement.

Walter Dean Myers, *Malcolm X: By Any Means Necessary.* New York: Scholastic, 1993. This reverent biography rightly emphasizes Malcolm's legacy as a role model. However, it tends to shy away from hard details on Malcolm's shortcomings, his bitter conflict with the Nation of Islam, and the controversy surrounding his murder.

Jack Rummel, *Malcolm X: Militant Black Leader.* New York: Chelsea House, 1989. A biography of Malcolm X with emphasis on his early life and development into an important leader; supplemented by numerous photos and an introductory essay by Coretta Scott King.

David Shirley, *Malcolm X.* New York: Chelsea Juniors, 1994. This relatively brief but balanced account of Malcolm X's upbringing, background, conversion to Islam, and philosophies, is complemented by a chronology and glossary of terms.

Jack Slater, *Malcolm X*. Chicago: Childrens Press, 1993. A short but well-illustrated text for the young adult that traces the life of Malcolm X, focusing mainly on his message and the reasons he chose to deliver it.

Works Consulted

Arnold Adofo, *Malcolm X*. New York: Crowell, 1970. An easily readable introduction to the life and times of Malcolm X.

Clayborne Carson, *Malcolm X: The FBI File*. New York: Ballantine Books, 1991. This is a valuable collection of primary-source material, documenting the files the FBI kept on Malcolm X. It is a great resource for historians and students of Malcolm X, as well as for anyone interested in the workings of the FBI.

Michael Friedly, *Malcolm X: The Assassination*. New York: Ballantine Books, 1992. This is the best recent book on the murder of Malcolm X. Friedly uses up-to-date information to reconstruct important events in the case, from the shooting to the motives of the Nation of Islam. A thoughtful, well-reasoned book, it is full of important source material. If students of the case read only one book, this should be it.

David Gallen, *Malcolm X: As They Knew Him*. New York: Carroll & Graf, 1992. Memoirs of Malcolm X, including reminiscences from Alex Haley, Maya Angelou, and James Baldwin. Of particular interest is the essay "Who Were the Killers?" by Maria Laurino of the *Village Voice*, which takes a look at the conspiracy theories of the assassination. Includes an excellent chronology of Malcolm's life.

Peter Goldman, *The Death and Life of Malcolm X*. New York: Harper & Row, 1973. This was the first important book written about the assassination of Malcolm X. Journalist Peter Goldman interviewed many involved in the case, and the book is still important today. Later works by other authors are based heavily on Goldman's excellent research and understanding of the case. Goldman was highly sympathetic to Malcolm X, and the book remains readable and interesting today.

Benjamin Karim, *Remembering Malcolm*. New York: Carroll & Graf, 1992. Benjamin Karim was Malcolm X's assistant minister at the New York's Mosque Seven. He left the Nation of Islam with Malcolm and was the man who introduced him that fateful day at the Audubon Ballroom. This is his reminiscence of Malcolm X.

Malcolm X, with Alex Haley, *The Autobiography of Malcolm X*. New York: Ballantine Books, 1964. When Malcolm X sat down with author Alex Haley, he told the story of his life, which Haley crafted into the book that is still the most important primary source for Malcolm X's life. This book traces Malcolm's life and thinking from his childhood through prison to the Nation of Islam to his break with the Black Muslims and ends shortly before his death. More than thirty years after it was written, it remains dynamic and is in its own way a classic American autobiography.

Jack Rummel Melrose, *Malcolm X: Militant Black Leader*. Los Angeles: Melrose Square Publishing, 1988. A look at the life of Malcolm X and his role as a radical in the African-American community.

Index

Picture Credits

Cover photos, clockwise from top: UPI/Bettmann, AP/Wide
World Photos, AP/Wide World Photos

AP/Wide World Photos, 17, 31, 32, 39, 40, 42, 43, 46, 61, 69, 75, 78

Archive Photos, 10, 19

Federal Bureau of Investigation, 72

© 1995 Christopher Smith/Impact Visuals, 81

UPI/Bettmann, 9, 12, 16, 20, 28, 29, 36, 47, 49, 54, 66, 70, 77, 82

UPI/Corbis-Bettmann, 13, 23, 26, 60

About the Author

Miriam Sagan holds a B.A. from Harvard University and an M.A. in writing from Boston University. Her books include *Women's Suffrage* from Lucent Books, *Tracing Our Jewish Roots* from John Muir Publishers, as well as numerous collections of fiction and poetry. Her work has also appeared in such magazines as *Ms., New Mexico Magazine, American Book Review, Family Circle, Mademoiselle,* and the *Christian Science Monitor.*